Love, Marriage . . . and Facebook

Love, Marriage . . . and Facebook

*Stories of Sex, Relationships,
and the Online Social Network
That's Changing All the Rules*

Marlo Gottfurcht

*Full Court Press
Englewood Cliffs, New Jersey*

Published in the United States of America
by Full Court Press, 601 Palisade Avenue
Englewood Cliffs, NJ 07632

Any similarity of characters in this book to actual
persons is purely coincidental.

ISBN 978-0-9846113-6-2
Library of Congress Control No. 2010941717

Book Design by Barry Sheinkopf for Bookshapers.com
(www.bookshapers.com)
Cover by Jen Curtis
Author Photograph by Lauren Fash
FCP Colophon by Liz Sedlack

THIS BOOK IS DEDICATED
To everyone who is married. . .
and on Facebook.

Table of Contents

Part Five

Falling in Like n' Love—Facebook Style

Acknowledgements

This book would never have happened had it not been for my dear friend Claudio. What started as a conversation over drinks has turned into a dream come true. Thank you for everything. . . our friendship, for believing in me and for letting me take this idea, run with it and never look back.

The Thank Yous:

The stories in this book are here because of you: the married people of Facebook. These personal and intimate stories inspired what you are about to read, and I hope they touch you as much as they touch me.

"The Beverly People," that connection is like no other.

Liz Topp, for the endless hours of helping me shape my ideas into some sort of logical form.

Jason Newman, my dear friend, "brother" and manager, who believed in my idea from day one. Thank you from the bottom of my heart. Now we just have to get you on Facebook.

Stephanie Simon, for your friendship and support.

Carmen, for saying yes.

Barry Sheinkopf, Book Shaper Extraordinaire, for your time, effort, patience, and incredible talent for taking my vision and turning it into reality.

Jen Curtis, for the best book cover ever.

Lauren Fash, for the magic behind the camera.

Erica Bardin and Susan Graham, my "cheerleaders," for your enthusiasm and bringing Erin Shea Brewer to life.

Dr. Rebecca Ishida, for your wisdom and help so early on.

The Ones That Matter: Adam D., Bryan B., Danny R., David S., Dominic S., Greg G., Jon and Julie A., Jon K., Leslie L., Lisa I., Lou P., Mike M., Ricki R., Stephanie C., and Stephanie M.

Extra special shout out to Derek, my great bff, and Ryan, for standing by me when I started this adventure.

Jill, my wonderful and dear friend, and the other El Rodeo Girls: Allison, Dayna, Kim, Lainie, Nicole, and Shani, for your everlasting friendship.

Alyson, a constant in my life. What a beautiful friend you are, inside and out, always and forever.

Gayle, my best friend. Your never-ending love and friendship mean the world to me.

Diz, I truly believe good things come to those who wait, and I'm so glad I waited (and believed in second chances). Our connection, laughs, great times, and incredible fun put a smile on my face every day. . .it's all good. I love making memories with you and can't wait for all of our tomorrows.

My brother Grant, what a lucky sister I am to have such a loving brother like you.

Petra, my Vieja, I will never forget you.

My mom, Sherry, and Stan, your love is pure, real, and unconditional. Thank you for all you do and being incredible parents.

My dad Elliot, a girl cannot get luckier in life to have a dad and friend like you. Thank you for all your love, strength, support, and guidance. I love you on top of the Empire State Building.

My ex-husband Greg, even though people don't get how an ex-husband and ex-wife can get along as we do, I'm proud to have shared almost half my life with you and to have the friendship we have today.

My two favorite people in the whole wide world, my beautiful kiddies, Casey and Tanner. You continue to inspire me and make me proud. I live for your smiles, laughter, cuddles, hugs, and kisses. Mama loves you more than you know.

To my over 600 friends on Facebook, the ones who made the difference, asked the questions, and had an impact on my life.

Preface

FOR BETTER OR FOR WORSE, for richer, for poorer, in sickness and in health, to love and to cherish. . .these are the things brides and grooms usually promise each other on their wedding day. But this is the twenty-first century, and those vows could use an upgrade. *To Facebook or not to Facebook?* Now *that* is the real question.

Facebook is the global leader in online social networking, with over 500 million active users, half of whom log on every single day. However, if you're also thinking that Facebook is full of college students, you're so stuck in 2005. These days, Facebook's fastest growing demographic is—wait for it—the older folk. We're talking over-thirty-five-year-olds, and especially women over fifty-five. There are more Facebookers between the ages of forty-five and sixty than between thirteen and seventeen. In other words, Facebook is full of married people. And many married people tend to have affairs. While precise numbers are famously hard to come by, a conservative estimate is that half of all married people will cheat on their spouses.

Many of these people have discovered that the Internet is the perfect tool to play around with extracurricular romance. It's a safe, relatively low-impact way to engage in sexy banter without the stress of being face-to-face or in real time on the phone. Many have found themselves typing things they would never have actually said out loud—frequently to old flames, high school boyfriends and girlfriends, favorite exes. Never before has it been so easy to reach out and establish a private, instant connection to nearly anyone from your past.

Most people who join Facebook don't know what they may be getting into. Online reunions with friends from years ago can make you feel young and restless, especially if you settled down years ago. Just as most people don't expect to get divorced, Facebook newbies often have a "no-harm, no-foul" attitude when, in fact, many roads that start on Facebook lead to major life changes, as demonstrated by the stories that appear in this book.

All around us, family, friends, and neighbors are grappling with their own stories, some of which are incredibly salacious. For example, one busy suburban soccer mom with a hectic schedule might never have bumped into her old high school sweetheart in person, but on Facebook, it was inevitable. Friendly online reunions like that happen all the time, and they can often lead to flirtatious emails that seem harmless enough. But then, it's late one night, a glass of wine in hand, husband out of town, and kids at a sleepover. Surely, it's OK to Facebook chat with her old boyfriend she hasn't seen in over two decades! Isn't it? What if the talk turns to how good the sex would be now? It's OK just to *speculate*, right? And from there, it's a slippery slope.

Not only is the content sensational, but the characters are ubiquitous. You may find it hard to believe, but these sorts of reunions, flirtations, and more are happening all around you, all the time. With phones, iPads, laptops, and nearly always available

Wi-Fi, the Internet and all its charms are accessible anywhere—even at 35,000 feet up in the air! Or in your high rise apartment building. Or your gated community. On your commuter train. Even at work. You may wonder if one of these characters is someone you know. Or you may wish he or she were you.

The irresistible and undeniable Facebook Effect is sweeping our nation's personal communications tools, sending shockwaves through many marriages. Therapists and marriage counselors are seeing more and more couples coming into their practice for help in resolving their conflicts involving marriage and Facebook. Rebecca Ishida, MFT, who has a private practice in Los Angeles and specializes in sex and love addiction and couples therapy, says, "Facebook has changed the landscape of reconnecting with people from your past. Facebook creates greater accessibility, opportunity, and immediacy for connection. Friendship, flirtation, and more are right at your fingertips."

Fidelity and deceit are recurring themes in any marriage, and people have been falling in and out of love for millennia; still, Facebook affects these themes and events in unprecedented ways. For example, can a Facebook dalliance translate into a real-life affair or more? (Answer: sometimes.) This book includes stories from across the spectrum, from getting it on to getting busted to getting back together.

Love, Marriage. . .and Facebook presents stories *inspired by* events from the front lines of the Facebook Effect. All names have been changed, and some details and facts adjusted, to protect the innocent (and the guilty). But their emotions are raw, and their stories pretty damn sexy. This book will get you hot, turn you on, and make you think twice, especially the next time you log onto Facebook.

Part One

Virtual Virgins:
Testing The Waters

IF YOU'RE NOT ON IT yet, you might be wondering: What's the whole point of Facebook, anyway? Sure, people use it to reconnect with people from their past, but *why*? It's not always about flirting, sex, or gossip. Maybe you are at a point in your life where being the dutiful wife and soccer mom just isn't enough, and you want and need more. Facebook can be an important outlet for aspects of your character that can't be expressed in any other way. Just keep in mind, Facebook is relatively public, and you sometimes don't know who's watching you.

In this section, you will find stories about people getting their feet wet with Facebook: from a single woman who refuses to flirt with a married man, to old high school friends getting reacquainted, to establishing Facebook codes to let your friends know you are getting laid. The seduction of Facebook always has to start somewhere.

1

Tales of a Fourth-Grade Something

THERE'S NOT MUCH OF a story to tell. . .yet.

This week someone found me on Facebook. He's a guy I went to grammar school with. We liked each other for a while, but, I mean, come on, we were in the fourth grade!

I remember checking in on Facebook from my phone and discovering that I had a friend request. I then saw Jordan's name. I actually laughed out loud! I hadn't thought about him in thirty years!

I accepted his friend request and wrote him a message. Since then we have caught up on everything. He is married with kids, and I am a divorced mom of three. When I told him of my marital "status" he commented to me:

Too bad I'm already married. LOL.

I was a little taken aback when he said that.

We chatted a few more times through the days and nights, and he said the comment again to me. . .twice.

I told him to be careful with Facebook. He was new on it. It can get tempting. There is harmless flirting, and maybe that's okay, but sometimes matters can go a step further. You need to make sure you draw the line in the sand and be careful not to cross it (unless that is your intention).

Call me crazy, but when a married man, like this guy, keeps telling a single woman, "Too bad I'm married," that is a sign in the wrong direction.

Despite my warnings, he keeps flirting with me.

How 'bout we meet for a drink one night?

Do you look the same as you did when you were younger? If so, then I'm in big trouble.

You mentioned you are having trouble falling asleep at night. I can suggest some "ways" to make you fall asleep.

Flirt after flirt after flirt. . .all as I'm telling him to be careful with Facebook. Yes, it's nice to be flirted with. But with a married man? I don't think so.

I know he is not the only married man (or woman for that matter) flirting on Facebook. I have talked to many of my friends, and they have told me some juicy stories.

Lots of shit goes down here on Facebook, apparently. Maybe I'll look into it, but certainly not with a married man.

Jordan is a friend, and it begins and ends there. He's a friend. That's it. All I do know is, if Facebook interferes with his marriage, it won't be from *this* Facebook friend.

2

Girls' Night Out: A Ladies' Perspective

August 2009

A GROUP OF SIX women are having dinner. They have all known each other since childhood. Four out of six are married. Three out of six have children. One out of six is separated.

One of the women poses a question: Do you think Facebook has caused problems in people's marriages? Or do you think the problem was present before Facebook came in the picture? The majority of the table feels Facebook isn't the problem. The problem had to exist before Facebook. They think Facebook is an excuse, *not* the problem.

Of the four married women, all had ex-boyfriends who were Facebook friends. Three said they had never had inappropriate conversations with any ex-boyfriends or male friends from the past. Two said their husbands see their Facebook pages, and that there is nothing to hide. One said her husband, who is not on Facebook, has a problem with it, so she is very careful who she friends and communicates with.

All the women but one could not believe people have Facebook sex. Of course, she's the one who has. All in all, these ladies have a lot to learn. . .on Facebook.

3

Double Life

I LIVE A DOUBLE LIFE. It's not really what you think. I'm not a CIA agent working undercover. Nor am I a gay man living in a heterosexual world. I have, and live, a double life on Facebook.

I'm a married man with two children. Married, I say. I don't say happily. I am a dutiful husband, bringing home the bacon, paying the bills, and playing the role I am supposed to be playing. On the outside, I am clean-cut, cultured, and conservative. But that's not me. . .not the *real* me.

Who *is* the real me? Just ask my friends on Facebook. I'm the one who makes people laugh, the one who posts the raunchi-est stuff I can find. I'm the one who pushes the limits and says the stuff we all think but are afraid to say. That's me. I'm that wild and crazy guy (good-looking too, I may add). And my wife has no idea.

I go to the office and do what I need to do. I own my own company and have the freedom to do as I please. The moment I leave the house and get in my office, I turn on the computer. Facebook is my first stop of the day. . .kind of like my morning coffee.

I have a following. My friends expect me to do the funny, make them laugh and think at the same time. The girls love me; the guys all want to be my friend. Yes, there are some I offend, and I do find each week that I get a few who defriend me. But what the fuck do I care? For all those who defriend, there are others who friend. I am not at a loss for Facebook friends.

My Facebook life is my secret life. My real-life friends with whom I am also Facebook friends know I am married. Those who don't know my personal life, let them guess. I do not publicize on Facebook that I am married. I have no marital status. I do post pictures of the kids, though, because they are my life and a huge part of me. As far as many people know, I am a single dad living the life.

My wife has no clue to this life of mine, no clue that I'm on Facebook. I use my real name, so yes, she could probably find out in a heartbeat. But she hasn't yet. Could I be more careful? Yes, but I'm not. So maybe I want to get caught and have her see the "real" me.

Is what I do on Facebook so bad? So what if I'm raunchy, dirty, and say it like it is? Is that a crime? No, but I have pushed the line. In fact, I have gone over that line, and once you take that leap, there's no going back.

I engage and interact with many people on Facebook. Of course, many of those people are women. Most of them are married, and some know I am. I have found that women want to be told certain things, want to hear certain things, when we Facebook chat. If a woman is in a horny mood, I know it, and she wants to hear you talk dirty to her. If a woman chats with me who just needs to vent about her fucking husband, well, I'm the sounding board she needs.

I know how to tell a woman she is beautiful and sexy just by typing the right words. I know how to tell a woman that she should put her hands between her legs and touch her wet pussy with her fingers. I know how to make a woman come just by typing. . .true fact, I have done it. This is the Facebook me. This, as I say, is the real me.

So is having Facebook sex crossing the line? Some might say yes, others no. I'm with the latter. When you take it a step further and meet the person, well, then one could argue that that is cheating. I have had a few drunken indiscretions, but that was a long time ago. To me, crossing the line is when an affair or flirt becomes emotional. To me, when the feelings hit the heart—well, there's no going back after that. I've come real close to that emotional feeling, and as unhappy I am with my wife, I can't get on that emotional level with someone until I leave my wife.

At first I thought I could handle this double life. I could do my thing every day, go to the office, be me, and then go home and be "the husband and father." At the end of the day, every day, I put my mask back on, go home to the pristine house, the home-cooked meal on the table, the squealing kids, and the cold, loveless wife. Yet the more I do this, the more I realize how difficult it is. I am not happy. I am not in a happy marriage, and I am tired of the double life.

I want to throw away the mask and be me all the time, 24/7. The real me is a good guy, a little dirty yes, but just around the edges. I have a real soft heart and just want to be happy. I know it's not easy to end a marriage, but it's even harder to pretend who you are. Day in and day out, I play a role I don't want to play anymore. I want to be me.

4

Lurking Assumptions

WHAT HAPPENS WHEN PEOPLE assume? We all know the saying: It makes an ass out of you and me.

People love to get into other people's business. They love gossip, and they love to know what is going on in everyone's lives. Many love to live vicariously though others—the married person living through the single person, the poor living through the rich. We all want to experience something that we are not.

The moment someone signs up for Facebook, regardless of their involvement or activity, they are allowing others to look into their lives. Those on Facebook want people to do so—the pictures of the kids, of the spouse, of themselves twenty pounds lighter. People love to sneak a peek. They feed off it and enjoy it.

I am one who loves Facebook. I update my status, at best, several times a week. I don't report every move I make (. . .is at the gym. . . .is eating dinner. . . .is taking a crap), but I do mention what's interesting (at least I think so).

People know some of my business. Not all. They know I was married. They know I have one kid. They know I am a MILF. They know I like to have fun and love my friends. They know just enough, or maybe too much.

As I said, we are all curious about others, and the curious brings out the lurkers. What's a "lurker"? Someone who lurks. Someone who watches, takes note, keeps quiet, but observes everything that is going on. Facebook is full of lurkers and many of them are my friends who lurk on my page.

I think the minute people became aware of my new marital status, they started to lurk. I didn't realize it until recently. A mom at my child's school, who is a Facebook friend, asked me if I was dating "x". She doesn't even know "x"; she just noticed how often "x" writes on my wall. That mom is a lurker.

I just ran into a friend I grew up with. She too knew about the change in my marital status (I'd never told her), and she too figured I was dating "x". How? From the friggin' wall-to-wall, back-and-forth, witty, cutesy, flirty comments we make. That friend is a lurker as well.

Just last week I updated my status that I was a happy woman. I had just had some good news on a project I was working on. Before I knew it, I had a ton of comments on my new status, and most of them assumed the happiness was due to "x". Why do people have to assume that the only reason a woman can be jumping up and down happy is because of a man?

So, to all you lurkers out there: You can continue to lurk. You can dissect every status update I make and try to figure them out. I'll even throw a few curve balls out there to fuck with you more. I'm gonna keep going, doing my thing, and you can have a hell of a time wishing you were me.

5

To Be Continued

HE WAS NEVER A guy I was attracted to. In fact, one of my closest high school friends always had a thing for him. We'd always been friends, hung out in the same crowd, more like brother and sister.

After high school, we went our separate ways. Actually, I didn't think of him that often. I married, had my kids, and did my thing. He didn't attend the twenty-year reunion, so truly he never crossed my mind.

After I joined Facebook, my marriage started to unravel. I found myself more on Facebook than in bed with my husband. I wasn't cheating on him—well at least, I don't consider Facebook-chatting late at night, with people of the opposite sex, cheating. After a while, we decided to end our marriage, and we separated.

I don't recall when, but at some point, I saw that my friend from high school had joined Facebook. We became friends, but I don't think we interacted at all. Again, he was not the one I was attracted to or the one I ever wanted.

I checked out his page and couldn't tell how he'd aged. He looked kinda cute, but he had a gorgeous girl on his arm and his status read "engaged," so I knew he was so off limits.

Time passed, and one day, I saw his picture pop up on my wall. I decided to check out his page again and noticed something. His picture had changed, and so had his status. He was now single.

What the fuck? I thought. So I emailed him. It was short, sweet, and to the point.

> *hey you! long time no talk. . .thought i would drop u a line and say hi. . .what are you up to? i thought i heard you were getting married. . .enjoy! let's talk soon.*

I knew he was single. . .I was just learning how to play the game.

He emailed me back within the hour, telling me he was no longer engaged (duh!), single, and ready to mingle. He told me about his work, his house, the usual catch-up. He works his ass off and was about to go on a long business trip. We exchanged the formalities, and said we should get together soon.

One night, late at night, he popped me up on chat. He was on the road, in his hotel, and we just started talking. It flowed. It was natural, as it had been back in high school, but better—more fun, more mature, more honest. The talk turned to flirting, and suddenly, I realized, I could like this guy.

He's a player, a true player. Yet there's something about him I like. He works hard, plays hard, and is dedicated, focused, and ambitious. He's a good guy with a good heart underneath all that bullshit player persona.

One conversation turned into another turned into another. All on Facebook chat. We talked life, we talked sex. We talked fantasies. We talked past, present, and future. After some time, I was done with this chat nonsense and wanted to take it a step further. I wanted to see him in person.

I waited and waited, but he didn't ask me out. He was always so noncommittal. Yes, we'll get together, he would say. When? I would ask. I knew he had a busy work schedule, but I also knew he went out. He told me of girls he picked up on. Told me of girls he hooked up with. I know we were friends, but I was starting to realize that that was the problem. He didn't take me seriously and only saw me as the girl from high school. That's the problem with this Facebook chat shit. We needed a face to face!

I finally asked him out. And he agreed.

The night before we were supposed to go out, I was Facebook-chatting with another friend from high school. He is married, with kids, and incredibly wise. He is also good friends with the guy I'm supposed to be going out with. We ended up having a three-way chat. I'm talking to both of them and they are talking to each other. And, of course, what's the topic of conversation? Our "date" for the following night. As flirty and forward as I was with this guy, I started getting the impression, from our mutual friend, that he didn't look at me "that way," that we were just friends. My wise friend told me to give it time and let my old high school chum get to know the new me, the real me. I listened to his advice and agreed.

The next day, I ended up going to the guy's house. We had wine and ordered in. And nothing happened. I was definitely attracted to him, but more than that, I loved and enjoyed our conversation, our laughs, and our interaction. Here was this "player" who did not play me, did not make a move on me. Yes, our conversations were sexual, but honest. Intimate, but true.

The night ended with a walk to the car and a kiss on the cheek. A kiss on the cheek? The kiss he gave me was definitely a little sister kinda kiss. He does look at me like a little sister, I realized. . .shit!

All the way home, I tried to analyze what had happened. He likes to fuck but doesn't want to fuck me. Is that a compliment? If I was just some random girl, we would have hooked up. I may be a girl, but I'm not random, for sure. So maybe not hooking up was a good thing. Maybe he thought more could happen, but at its own pace.

The next morning he popped me up on Facebook, told me how great I looked, that we needed to do it again. So maybe, just maybe, he could get over this brother/sister bullshit and can start looking at me as the woman I am.

What happens now? I typed on chat. *This is only chapter one of our story. What happens next?*
To Be Continued. . . he replied.
To Be Continued.

6

Who The Hell Is Happy, Anyway?

ONE OF MY CLOSE friends just told me they were getting divorced. Why? Because they were unhappy. Guess what my response was? Who the fuck is happy anyway? If you ask my husband, or me, we would both say that we are unhappy. I mean, who the hell is truly happy in their marriage these days? Marriage and happiness. . .a totally oxymoron. Maybe the happiness is there in the beginning, but once you do the deed and have kids, things fuckin' change!

This same friend, the soon-to-be divorcee, also told me I should go on Facebook. I was hesitant at first, but I was starting a business and thought it could help. I could totally use it for a networking tool. That's it. Networking only. Yet networking was not working, and I got hooked. I didn't think I would be into it at all, and I used to tease my friend about how many hours she spent on it. Now, I get it, totally get it, and I probably have her beat!

I am on Facebook all the time and love it. My husband works late a lot and travels too, so Facebook is a way for me to escape it all. Once my kids go to bed, I pour a glass of wine and settle down for some Facebook.

Back to my marriage: I love my husband, and he loves me. But come on, *happy*? Not a chance. We are both products of divorce, and it would never be an option for me. I will live unhappy—I don't care.

Facebook has helped me with those unhappy times. Those times I just feel like wringing my husband's neck. I like to chat a lot online, especially with my friends. I know we can just pick up the phone and call each other, but it's more fun this way. Plus I think that, when we type and chat, there are no "rules." For example, just the other day I told a friend of mine that she should go and invest in a new vibrator.   I don't think I would ever be able to tell her that in person; in fact, I know I could never. I am much more bolder in my typing.

Several of my ex-boyfriends are on Facebook. There is one special one I like to chat with. My husband knows we are friends (by the way, my husband is *not* on Facebook. Why the hell not? What does he have to hide?), but my husband does not know we chat. Any time I see this certain ex online, we talk. We flirt. We totally flirt. He is married too, and I know, we both know, that this thing stops at flirting.

Why won't it go further? I would never cross that line. I would never let anything like that ruin my marriage. The ex-boyfriend just gives me an outlet. Chatting to him makes me happy, makes me feel wanted and pretty. It brings me back to a time I was me—not a mom or a wife.

I mean, come on, we are not having Facebook sex, for God's sake, we just chat and say it like it is. I actually know a few people who *do* have Facebook sex. Sounds pretty awesome, I might add, but it's not me. No way. Flirt-chatting with the ex is the closest I will do to whoring it up. I am doing nothing wrong, and neither is he. It's refreshing, it's totally innocent. I will forever stay married to my husband, unhappy and all. Who the fuck cares as long as I have my Facebook.

7

The Beetle Has Landed

A GROUP OF US met for dinner one night: two men and four women. We all went to high school together and have known each other from even before that. In the age of Facebook, we had all reconnected and wanted to have a fun night to catch up.

Of the six of us, three were married, one was newly separated and two had never been married. Only two of us had children. We were all heading towards forty but looked more like thirty.

In the middle of the conversation, a large bug flew into the hair of one of the women. One of the men helped her get it out. It was a big bug, disgusting in fact, and looked like a beetle.

As the drinks flowed and the conversation came easy, attention turned to the one who was newly separated. It was intriguing to the ones that were married—not so much to the single ones.

"Have you slept with anyone else yet?" asked one of the men.

"No. Not yet," the newly separated one answered.

"Well, you need to let us know when you do. We want to know all about it and how it was. You'll have to update your Facebook status to let us know," replied the same man.

"I'm not going to broadcast on Facebook when I have sex!" she said.

"Then you can do it in code," the same man replied back.

"What would I say?" asked the woman.

The other man looked up, the one who had taken the bug out of the women's hair. "Just write, *The beetle has landed*. That's your code, and then we'll know. *The beetle has landed*," he repeated.

And so our group of six decided that the newly single woman would update her status to let us all know when the beetle had landed.

8

Lost and Found

WHO AM I? I am a woman. I am a mother. I am a daughter and sister. I am a wife. Who am I? I ask again. I am all these things, yes, but who am I *really*? I'm not getting existential at all, but seriously, who am I?

I am the one who puts the dinner on the table, folds the laundry, and cleans the house. I am the one who helps with the homework, book reports, and endless projects. I am the one who drives on field trips, takes and picks up from school and carpools. I am the one who is the glue that holds this family together. I am the one who makes sure everyone is happy. . .but me.

Sometime between getting married and having kids, I got lost, in the figurative sense. I lost who I was. I became the dutiful wife and then, of course, the hands-on mother. Sometime between saying "I do" and hearing "It's a girl," I forgot who I really was.

It took years to realize that I had lost my identity. It wasn't until my kids were in school full-time, and I didn't need to cater to their every whim and need, that I stopped and realized I was lost. Yes, I remained "Super Mom," but my kids had an independence by then, which gave me a few minutes every day to breathe and think and wonder and ponder. Where was my identity? Where had I lost it, and could I find it again?

Reclaiming your identity isn't an easy task. You don't post signs in your neighborhood asking for a reward to anyone who can find your identity. It's not on the back of a milk carton or on *America's Most Wanted*. Finding your identity is a personal task, one you can only perform when you are ready and willing. Of course, there are some outside forces that can help. . .for me the one that counted was a little thing we call Facebook.

I'd never have thought that this immensely popular social networking site would be the one to help me reclaim who I was. I signed up as innocent as the next person and never expected the ride that I was about to take.

It started innocently enough, but what started to happen is what helped me find "me." Friend after friend who friended me or I friended (are you following this?) was someone who made an impact on my life. . .my childhood best friend, my camp bunk mates, my first kiss, my first "first." All of these people made me remember. The conversations, the memories, the "remember when's," all came flooding back. And slowly but surely, so did my identity. Oh, so *that's* who you are. You've been gone so long, I hardly recognized you.

Some of my friendships were closer, more intimate, than others—not in the sexual sense, but in the deep, meaningful conversation sense. These conversations made me think, made me wonder and ask questions about myself.

As I slowly reacquainted myself with my identity, I soon began to realize that the person I was, and the situation I had been in, were not happy. My newly reclaimed identity made me happy, and that identity and the current life I'm living could not comingle. I realized that my role as a wife was not where I wanted to be. I had not been happy for a long time, through all the meals, the cleaning, the car pools. I was merely going through the motions and not enjoying them.

I don't blame my husband. I don't blame myself. I think things just happen and when you marry young—there is a risk of it not working out as you get older. My husband is an incredible father, and for that I am blessed. We just were not incredible as a couple, as a husband and wife, as one.

We separated, and I knew it would be permanent. I had my Facebook, my friends, and my support system. I developed friendships with people I never would have had as a Mrs. For the first time, in a long time, I felt a weight off my shoulders, and I had a big smile on my face. I felt empowered, powerful, and strong. I knew the road ahead might be bumpy, but I knew I had friends, hundreds of them, to lean on, when I needed a hand.

And so, with my identity firmly grasped with a hard grip (I'm never gonna let it go again), I am ready for my future: excited, willing and ready.

Part Two

Foreplay to Fucking
The Facebook Way

FACEBOOK IS THE ULTIMATE uninhibitor and, under the right circumstances, an aphrodisiac. People who are too shy for phone sex get intimate on Facebook chat every day. There you are, in your own comfortable den, sipping a glass of wine, all by yourself, when your hottest old flame pops you up and wants to know if you still have your old cheerleader outfit. Ten minutes later, you could be typing things you would never say out loud.

Then there are people who throw themselves into Facebook sex with abandon. After all, it can be a really enjoyable, relatively innocent, utterly safe sexual outlet. Because it's remote and there are hardly ever any strings attached, Facebook makes it easy to have raunchier, more explicit sexual experiences than you might enjoy in your married life. Just like there are better and worse lovers, there are highly skilled online sexers who often end up pushing the limits of technology and fidelity.

The stories start off tame, people who think they're not breaking any rules, just bending them—from the man who has a spontaneous Facebook threesome to the woman who finds out her high school love still has the vibrator he bought her twenty years earlier.

And now to the good stuff: Tame is fine. . .but raunchy is even better. Get ready to get hot, heavy, and turned on! In one story, two housewives get down and dirty with each other; in another, two parents (married to others) on a movie play date use Face-book chat at its naughtiest. These people really push the techno-logical envelope.

9

Cooking and Fertilizing

BE HONEST. DO YOU swing more toward the Farmville crowd, or do you like the chefs in Café World? Anyone who is active on Facebook knows that never a day goes by without a gift sent or neighbor request from one of those goofy games. I swore I would never get into them. . .until my friendship with JD started.

JD and I grew up together. We had the same friends, hung out, but there was never anything romantic between us. He has been my Facebook friend from the beginning, and at our twenty-year high school reunion we caught up on our lives and the journeys we had taken.

About a year after a reunion, JD's marriage fell apart. He was getting divorced. I *was* married—but not happily. I felt myself turning more and more to Facebook instead of dealing with the issues at home. JD and I were becoming close, and we both felt, but never admitted aloud, a mutual attraction.

One night I was chatting online with JD. He told me to hang on because he had to put food on the stoves in his Café World. What the fuck was he talking about? He told me about Café World, and he said he would send me an invite to be his neighbor.

I had seen these games on Facebook but never had any desire to even go there. Facebook was addictive enough; why in the hell would I want to start worrying about what food I was cooking?

JD was convincing enough, though, and I decided to try it. Can't hurt, right?

Right away, it became competitive with us. He was way ahead in the game, and I was just beginning. He would tell me what to do, what dishes to make, and how to fix up my Café in order to get the most points. And yes, the inevitable happened: I got addicted.

Soon enough, every time I logged onto Facebook, I checked out my Café. I started timing what dish to make to when I would be back at home to serve it to my customers. And JD loved it. He loved the competition.

One night, we were both on late and were working on our Café's. He said something, I said something, and all of a sudden he put a wager out.

> JD: *I'm so good at this game. I have you beat!*
> Me: *Not for long.*
> JD: *I tell you what. . .let's make this interesting. I'll give you one week. . .I bet you that you can't catch up to me.*

Me: *So simple to do. What are we betting?*

JD: *If you win, I'll do anything you want. If I win, you do what I want.*

Me: *It's a bet.*

I never really stopped to think what I would have JD do; I was in it more for the competition. He was so fucking cocky that he could beat me at this game, and I was not gonna let him.

As the week went by, I was jamming. He had one night that he had to go away on business, so it gave me an advantage, since he wasn't online. I was gonna win this thing.

Three days before the competition was supposed to end, I logged onto Facebook and got a neighbor request from him from Farmville. Another fucking game.

Me: *What the fuck JD? You can't bring Farmville into the mix.*

JD: *Oh yes I can. Double or nothing. Sunday, 11 p.m. Whoever is winning both games, gets it all.*

Me: *All?*

JD: *All. Trust me. You want it all.*

Me: *Oh, I do, do I?*

JD: *Trust me.*

So I started to wonder. . .do I really try and win this thing, or do I let him win and see what he wants me to do to him? We were very flirty, and although I was still officially married, it was slowly coming to an end. JD was incredibly attractive to me and fuck it,

I would do something with him. I would totally do something with him.

I decide to work my ass off in my Café. Give him a run for his money. With Farmville, I just let it ride. Whoever wins that one, I thought, wins. Slowly but surely I was catching up with him, redecorating my Café, serving everything from Peking duck to halibut to *carne asada*. I'm cooking like a master. I am the Iron Chef of Café World.

As for Farmville, he sent me a sheep. I sent him a cow. This went back and forth. We planted pumpkins and wheat, fertilized each other's plants, and fed the chickens. It was getting hot over here in Farmville.

On Sunday night at 11 p.m., we met online to chat. The whistle has blown and the game was over. Who was the winner, and what was the prize?

> JD: *Okay. Game over. Don't look. Don't check and see*
> *who won. Not yet.*
> Me: *What are you waiting for? You scared?*
> JD: *No. Just building the momentum.*
> Me: *Fuck the momentum. Let's get to it.*

So at the count of three, we both logged onto Café World first. I was the winner, ever so slightly, but I'd won. Victory.

> JD: *Wow. You beat me. Ok, I'll accept that. You played*
> *well and fair. But let's see what Farmville has to say.*

Again we counted to three and log onto Farmville. He'd won.

> JD: *Well, lookie here.*
>
> Me: *I felt bad I was beating you in Café World, so I let you win here.*
>
> JD: *I'm sure you did. So it's a tie.*
>
> Me: *Yes it is. A tie. What do we do about that?*
>
> JD: *Well, I know what I want from you. Do you know what you want from me?*
>
> Me: *Still contemplating.*
>
> JD: *Then let me go first.*
>
> Me: *Fair enough.*
>
> JD: *Okay. . .here goes. I want you. I want to learn more about you, your body. I want to explore you.*

I was speechless.

> JD: *Since I can't have you right now, I want you the next best way. On here, right now. I want to make love to you right here, right now.*

I said nothing.

> JD: *You still there?*
>
> Me: *Yeah. Just. . .I don't know. . .*
>
> JD: *Does that turn you off, what I asked of you?*
>
> Me: *I think that's what shocks me the most. . .it doesn't.*
>
> JD: *Wow. . .*

Me: *Wow is right.*

JD: *So have you figured out what you want from me?*

Me: *I think I want the same.*

JD: *Let me check in the rule book if both winner's can ask for the same prize. . . Yup, it's OK. You are clear.*

Me: *Lol.*

JD: *I'm serious. All games aside—*

Me: *But you love the games.*

JD: *I do. But how I feel about you is not a game.*

Me: *I know.*

JD: *Do me a favor. Take off your clothes. All of them.*

And so I do.

JD: *I want to feel you. Tell me how you are feeling.*

Me: *Wet.*

JD: *Man, that's good. Real good.*

Me: *Hey. . .you're not the only winner here. I get some, too! Take it all off.*

And so he does.

Me: *What are you feeling?*

JD: *Hard.*

The rest is history. The two of us, Ms. Wet and Mr. Hard, two friends on Facebook and neighbors on Café World and Farmville, spent the rest of the night collecting our prizes over and over again.

10

I Still Have the Vibrator
I Bought You When You Were Sixteen

JUSTIN AND I WERE high school sweethearts. I always thought he was the one I was going to marry, but as time passed and we grew older, we both met other people and realized we were not meant to be.

I think, in the back of our minds, we still had a thing for each other. I used to have this fantasy that we would meet up again. There we would be in the market, in the produce section, and run into each other. We would discover that we were both divorced and we would end up back together.

We lived in the same city, but our paths rarely crossed. As soon as I joined Facebook, though, he was one of the first people I looked for. At first he was not on—and then one day he joined and I friended him.

One Sunday night, my husband was out of town. I was having a glass of wine and settled in for some late night Facebooking. I don't know why, but I decided to send Justin a private message. Our Facebook contact had been at a minimum, but something made me want to reach out to him that night. I did, and within minutes he responded. We decided to move our messaging to Facebook chat.

Half an hour later, there we were, chatting away. One thing led to another, and the chat became intimate. Another glass of wine later, it *really* became intimate. We had not been "with" each other for almost twenty years.

We had been so young, and each other's "first's," so inexperienced. We talked about what it would be like now. . . probably insane. Yes, the sex would be insane. I mean, come on, isn't it normal to think about that?

Now that we were older and experienced, what would it be like to be with your "first" again? We would both know what we were doing, where to touch, where to explore. It gave me chills just thinking about it.

I confided to him that my sex life with my husband was mediocre at best.

Do you use a vibrator? he asked.

What do you mean? Me alone or us together? I replied.

Both of you. . .together, he said.

No, in all honestly, we don't, I replied.

Well, you should. By the way, I still have the vibrator I bought for you when you were sixteen, he told me.

What? First of all, *gross!* Second of all, I barely had a memory of him getting or using a vibrator in our relationship.

Don't you remember? I bought it for us, and you were so shy. I think you let me use it on you once. I still have it in a box somewhere. . .why, I don't know. It's just there with other stuff from that time. Anyways, you should get one. A vibrator, I mean. I recommend the pocket rocket. You will love it, he told me.

Thanks, ex-boyfriend of mine. Thanks for the vibrator recommendation.

So, here's the question of the night: If an ex-boyfriend admits that he still has the sex toy he used on you twenty years ago, it must mean he has some fantasy thoughts about you, right? I thought about this and I have to say I was a little turned on by it. The wine helped—but, I admit, getting turned on by your first love is a good feeling.

Although it was a computer and a keyboard that separated us, we both knew what the next step was. And it was at that point that we ventured down the path. . .Facebook sex.

Facebook sex? Is there such thing? There's real sex. There's phone sex. There's Skype sex. There's even sexting, right? Facebook had to be as good as all of the above. Maybe not as good as the real thing, but you only live once, and opportunities sometimes come up that will never come up again. He was at the office, my husband was out of town, and it was long past midnight. . .sounds like the planets were aligned, and there was no time like the present.

We started to chat dirty to each other. I told him how I re-membered his body, his touch. He said the same to me. He told me to touch myself and I told him to touch himself. And there we were. . .two people. . .old loves. . .touching our bodies and remem-bering what it was like to be with each other.

It got incredibly hot and heavy, and I was wetter than I had been in a long time. He typed that he had come, but I was not there yet. I wasn't sure I could finish the task at hand while one-handedly typing on the computer and decided to do so in my bed, once we got off chat.

We ended up saying our goodbyes, and I have to say that night, in the privacy of my own room, I never made myself come as hard as I did.

The next morning, I texted him a simple text. . .one word that said it all. . .

Wow!

Justin's words and thoughts lingered with me all week. We chatted a few times after that, but we never shared a night like that again. I'm fine with the fact that it was sort of like a one-night Facebook stand because I know it will happen again. That chance encounter, whether it's on Facebook or in the produce sec-tion of the market, we will have it again. And by the way, he was right. . .the pocket rocket is the best!

11

Phat Chat

I'T'S 3:02 A.M., and I can't sleep. My wife and kids are upstairs fast asleep, and I'm downstairs, in my den, watching ESPN highlights. My laptop sits in front of me, and I am reminded that I need to send off a work email. I do it and, before I shut the computer down, I log onto Facebook.

I'm a Facebook junkie in the sense I like it, use it, and find it a fun form of entertainment. Usually, I'm on it during the day while at the office, not so much at home. I can honestly say I have never been on it at *this* time of the night. There's probably not much going on anyways, but I thought I would take a look.

As soon as the home page comes on, I see that I actually have a few friends that are on, too. Man, I had no idea that people come on here this late at night. A few guys, a distant cousin back East. . .and a few women I know. . .one from high school and one from college.

I decide to start the chat with the one from high school. Let's call her Girl #1.

> Me: *Hey stranger. . .what are you doing up so late?*
> Girl #1: *hey u! long time no talk. . .the question is what are u doing up so late?*
> Me: *One of those nights. . .can't sleep.*
> Girl #1: *i hear u. . .me too.*

The chitchat goes back and forth—very casual and very, very innocent. Suddenly I get a pop up from the girl I went to college with. Let's call her Girl #2.

> Girl #2: *You have some explaining to do, being up so late!*
> Me: *I'm just doing my thing, girl. . .what's your story?*
> Girl #2: *Girls' night out, and I came home to a sleeping house. I'm wide-awake and still—*
> Me: *Wasted.*
> Girl #2: *LOL! Yes, wasted! Wanna come over? I'll show you just how wasted I am.*

Girl #2 is coming onto me. She hasn't changed much since college.

> Girl #1: *u still there? u didn't fall asleep on me, did u?*
> Me: *Nope, still here.*
> Girl #1: *good. . .thought i lost u for a sec. . . having fun*

talking to u. i was just remembering when we made out at that party in 9th grade. . .u were always a great kisser.

Girl #1 is coming onto me. She hasn't changed much since high school.

Here I am. . .married father of three, and I have these two women. . .both still hot as fuck, and they are both coming onto me. I quietly shut the door to my den, lock it in fact, and get comfy on my couch. I think I'm gonna settle down with some Facebook fun.

> Girl #2: *OMG. . .You would love to see me right now.*
> Me: *Why?*
> Girl #1: *u were always such a babe. heh-heh.*
> Girl #2: *I'm wearing actually. . .nothing. I'm wearing nada. Wanna come over, or did I already ask you that?*
> Me to #2: *Nothing, huh? Don't tempt me.*
> Me to #1: *A babe? LOL! You were always the girl I had at 14 but could never get when it really mattered.*
> Girl #1: *u could have had me whenever u wanted. . . still ;-)*
> Girl #2: *Guess where my hand is now?*

OK, I have been on here for what, twenty minutes, a half hour? These women are fucking horny at 3 a.m. This is totally uncharted water for me. Not something I do, but something I have heard my buddies talk about. I don't consider it cheating, just heavy, heavy flirting. The only touching I'm gonna do is to myself, so what's the harm with a little dirty talk. Plus, bonus! Two women at the same time, and they don't even know. Couldn't think of a better way to spend the middle of the night! Let's roll!

> Me to #2: *You want the PG, R or X version of where I think your hand is?*
> Girl #2: *XXX. . .is that an option?*
> Me to #1: *I could have u whenever I wanted?*
> Girl #1: *and still. . .that's the most important part.*
> Me to #2: *Your hands are in your wet, luscious pussy.*
> Girl #2: *Fuck! You almost made me come with that response. Give me more!*
> Me to #1: *OK, then, I'd want you bent over with my dick in your vagina.*
> Me to #2: *Take those fingers and fuck yourself like it's my cock going in and out.*
> Girl #2: *MMMM. . ..I am so wet. I wish you could feel me.*
> Girl #1: *i love feeling your cock in me.*
> Me to #2: *I'm so hard right now. My dick is so hard.*

At this point, I think cut and paste will suffice.

> Me to #1: *I'm so hard right now. My dick is so hard.*

And so it goes, back and forth, back and forth. Me and #1; Me and #2. Both have their fingers in them, riding themselves as if it was me. Me? I'm taking care of myself, one-handed typing and all, as I let the girls have their pleasure.

As soon as our business is done, I say goodnight and thank you to both #1 and #2. It is 3:48 and *now* I am ready to sleep.

12

I Want to Make You Come So Hard Your Ears Will Ring

AM I READING WHAT I think I just read? I had to repeat it out loud because I couldn't believe Mike actually typed that:

> Mike: *I want to make you come so hard your ears will ring.*

Wow! I can honestly say I don't know if a guy has ever said that to me, on Facebook or in person.

Mike and I shared a drunken kiss one night in college, ages ago, but that's about as far as our romance went. We lost touch through the years and reconnected on Facebook, like everyone else I know. We became pretty close Facebook friends, consistently emailing, commenting on each other's status, and of course doing a little harmless flirting.

We both have kids and are happily married in different states. In fact, we live far enough away from each other to make Facebook flirting sessions incredibly innocent because an in-person meeting would be pretty much impossible.

One night he pops me up. He tells me he is away on a business trip and alone in his hotel room. Hmm. I'm used to flirting with him, but this is a little more information than he usually shares. I'm not sure where this is going, but I have an idea.

I love my husband dearly, but we have been married for an awfully long time and are not really getting high scores for our sex life, if you know what I mean. We have "spouse sex"—same ol' thing each time around. That is, we have spouse sex on the rare occasion that we actually get around to doing it at all. So when my friend Mike takes the flirting a little further, it excites me.

> Mike: *I'm all alone. . .and thinking of you. You do know I always think about you. . .*

So what do I do? Do I go for it or run for the hills? A few deep breaths later, I decide to go for it. There's always a first for something, right? I don't consider this cheating. What's the worst that can happen? If I don't like it, then I'll just never do it again, right? I tell myself to stop being so fucking analytical and just do it. So I do. . .

> Me: *You're all alone and thinking of me. . .what are you thinking about?*

Mike: *Your hot little body next to mine.*

Me: *I like that.*

Mike: *Do you, now? Wanna know what I would do to that hot little body of yours?*

Me: *Tell me.*

And away we go. . .

Mike: *First I would take you in my arms and kiss you. Slowly I would kiss you. . .over and over again. I would then take off your top and spend my time caressing and licking your breasts. One by one, over and over. I would trace my tongue across your nipples and feel your hardness. I would then take my hands and move them down your body, taking off your panties. My fingers start to explore you . . .all around, deeper and deeper.*

Whoa! This is getting incredibly interesting. I admit I am getting turned on. He knows what he is doing. He pauses in the typing, and I guess that means it's my turn. But what to say? Here goes nothing!

Me: *Can you feel how wet I am?*

I'm a firm believer that less is more!

Mike: *Oh, baby. . .I am so hard now. You are so wet. I*

just want to be inside of you.

Me: *I want you inside me.*

Mike: *I put my cock in your pussy and it feels so damn good. You are so wet. . .Oh, baby . . .mmmmmm. . . Can you feel how good it feels? Come on baby, I just want you to come.*

Me: *Mmmm. . .you feel so good. So good. . .*

Mike: *I want to make you come so hard your ears will ring.*

I can honestly say that nobody ever, ever, ever has said something like that to me. Husband, boyfriend, lover. . .no one. Where do these guys come up with this lingo? I'm not even sure if it turns me on. I'm enjoying this back and forth, don't get me wrong, but coming so hard that my ears will ring? That's a new one.

This goes on for a few more minutes. My hands are down my pants, but he's more into it than I am. I know he is about to finish when he types. . .

Mike: *I'm gonna come. Where do you want it? Mouth, tummy, tits, or inside.*

No one has ever asked me that either. They just do it where they want to. I actually get a choice, virtual though it may be. I spin the wheel of come in my head and it lands.

Me: *My tits. Come all over my tits.*

There's a pause on the other end for a minute or two.

> Mike: *That was incredible, sweetheart. You were incredible!*

I was? I didn't do that much, I thought. It was the easiest sexual experience I ever had.

We chat for a few more minutes and then say our goodbyes. I don't feel guilt; I don't feel bad I shared that with him. As I said, I love my husband dearly, and I simply chalk this up as another experience. I'm still horny when I say goodbye to Mike, so my husband is the one who gets lucky. If he only knew what made me come so fast when we made love that night!

Mike and I still talk and flirt often on Facebook. Once in a while we will refer to what happened, but usually we don't make much mention of what went down. Once in a while, I wonder if we will do it again. Or maybe, I will do it again with someone else. And why not? That night, everyone was a winner!

13

Let's Fuck

THERE'S NOTHING LIKE GETTING fucked on Facebook. I'm talking about the fuck we all love and know and can't get enough of. Getting fucked is great, but getting fucked on Facebook— well, don't knock it until you've tried it.

What starts as a friendly Facebook chat turns to flirting and, sometimes, just sometimes, to more. I say something, he says something, and the rest is history—no strings attached, no physical contact. I can be in my PJs, hair up, zit cream on, and still have a fanfuckingtastic orgasm.

I don't know why, but once you hit forty on Facebook you get flirted with all the time. I've been propositioned by all sorts of guys: married, single, divorced. . .you name it, I have had it. They all know I'm a married soccer mom with two kids; but I guess, since they don't know my husband, they don't care. And I don't care either! I don't think it's cheating. I enjoy and need it in my life.

My most regular Facebook Fuck is Frankie. We grew up together and rekindled our friendship on Facebook. He's an amazing guy. Married with a kid, Frankie and my virtual relationship was strictly platonic—at first.

Frankie travels frequently for work, and sometimes he's in another time zone. I always have Facebook open on my computer, whether I'm actually looking at it or not. So Frankie tends to notice that I am on a lot. We have had many conversations, late night, early morning, even middle of the day. Our chats run from the mundane to the gossipy and, finally, the erotic. He's asked me what my favorite position is. I've asked him how important it is to swallow.

I can't remember how our usual flirty conversation turned into virtual sex. He told me how good I looked the last time we ran each other, and how he had been looking forward to getting back to his hotel room and seeing if I was online. I told him I loved our chats too, and that he didn't look so bad himself. It was some time after this banter that he took it to the next level.

Frankie: *Fuck. . . I'm getting hard just talking to you.*

I was pretty new to virtual sex, so I didn't know how to take it at first. I thought, Is he joking? Is he just messing around? How should I respond? In the same vein, I assumed.

Me: *Oh, are you now? I admit it, I'm feeling tingly.*

Before I knew it, I was naked, spread eagled, typing with one hand and finger fucking myself until I came.

Since that day, Frankie and I do this quite often. It has only stayed on Facebook and has never crossed over into reality. I have seen him once, face to face, since our Facebook affair started. It was a social situation. When we hugged, spouses by our side, we squeezed a little longer, tighter and harder than usual. We don't intend to take it into reality, and it's something we both love and look forward to. No harm, no foul, right?

My first Facebook Fuck was with Billy. We dated in high school and have been in touch, on and off, through the years. We became Facebook friends but never interacted—no emails, chats, or wall posts. One late night we were both on, and he popped me up. I had a glass of wine in me, and our talk turned pretty provocative. One thing led to another, and he told me to play with myself. So I did. And he did. And it was pretty damned hot. We are still Facebook friends, but it never happened again—a true FONS (Facebook One Night Stand).

I've had other Facebook Fucks. Are they all the same? Well, considering I am doing the fucking myself, yeah, it's the same. Some of the guys use different words, different language. Some type more. Some type less. Some tell me step by step what they are doing.

> Him: *I am taking off my pants. I am touching myself.*
> *My dick is so hard. It's in my hands and it's throbbing.*

Others just moan.

Him: *Mmmmmm. Ohhhhh. Yeah, baby. . . . . . Mmmm-mmmmmmm.*

Some tell me what they want to do to me.

Him: *I want to put you against the wall. Pull your hair to the side and kiss your neck. I want to smell you . . .*

While others just say what's on their mind, without any thought for making it original or even creative.

Him: *Let's fuck.*

Sometimes it can get humorous, and sometimes outside forces cause a Facebook Fuck Buzz Kill. For example, I was once having Facebook sex with someone when a friend kept popping me up to chat. Another time, Frankie and I were getting it on and my daughter, who is my Facebook friend, kept popping me up from her friend's house. Buzz to the kill!

Phones ring, doorbells chime, spouses walk through the door unexpectedly. All that can ruin a fuck, but that's part of the risk. My partners and I always, always Clear Chat History. It's the virtual way of how to practice safe Facebook sex. The last thing I need is for my kids to see my last conversation with Frankie (or Kevin, Tony, Bobby. . .) and ask me, "Where did you go, Mom?" when they see I've written *I'm coming.*

So is the life on Facebook. It's not all innocent and pristine.

It's what you make of it and it works for me. What's better than virtual cock? No hairy balls. No mess to clean up. I get the real one at home and one real cock is more than enough for me.

14

A New Way to Watch a Movie

IT WAS ONE OF those holidays when the kids and I were home. They had to be entertained. You know those days. They were dying to go to the movies, and I didn't mind taking them. I wanted to make good with the wife, so I told her to take the day off. I would take care of the kids. If I was her hero, maybe, just maybe, I would get some that night.

As we were standing in line for popcorn, my kids ran into some friends. They were with their mom. I knew her, but not very well. Our kids had grown up together. She had always caught my eye—an attractive MILF for sure. The kids were excited to see one another and decided they wanted to sit away from the grownups in the front row. I understood. I'd been a kid once too and done the same thing.

The kids went to their seats, leaving us alone, so we sat together. The theater was not crowded at all, and we were far from the kids, sitting in the back.

The small talk commenced. We covered how the kids were doing in school, what we thought of the new principal, what sports the boys were going to do that spring, all the usual parent talk. Then Facebook came up. I told her I was active on it, as was she. She got out her phone to friend me right there and then. I got out mine and accepted.

The lights dimmed, and we knew the talking had to end. I still had my phone in my hand and I decided to chat with her via Facebook.

Me: *Hey, friend.*

She looked down at her phone, saw it was me who sent the message and smiled.

Her: *Hey, friend.*
Me: *What do you think of the movie?*
Her: *Lol! It hasn't even started yet!*
Me: *I have a feeling it's gonna be a long 2½ hours!*
Her: *LOL!*
Me: *I can think of many other ways I could spend my time.*
Her: *Oh, really, now. . . .*

At that point, I looked at her. She met my gaze. It was a look I will never forget. I hadn't seen anything like it in a while—probably the last time had been back in college: the look that flirts with you, the look that undresses you with her eyes, that says, *I'm wet between my legs*, that pleads with you to do something about it. You know the look I'm talking about.

> Me: *Wouldn't you like to know.*
> Her: *Try me. . .I'm game.*

Shit! This MILF was playing it right back at me. I started off slow.

> Me: *You look pretty sexy there. . .*
> Her: *You're not so bad yourself. . .pretty fucking hot.*

The kids were far, far away in the front row, and there was hardly a soul near us.

> Me: *I am so hard right now.*

She looked down at my lap and saw the bulge coming out of my pants.

> Her: *That was quick, LOL.*
> Me: *That's about the only thing that's quick about me.*
> Her: *Well, why don't we find out.*

She turned to take something out of the purse on the seat next to her.

Her: *Put your hand in your pants and let me see how hard you really are.*

I didn't waste any time. The pressure of my jeans against my cock was intense. I shifted in my seat and unzipped my pants. I had my cock in one hand and my phone in the other.

Me: *I want to see you touch your wet pussy.*

She lifted her skirt and parted her g-string to show me her lips were showing. It was then that I realized what she had taken out of her purse—a fucking vibrator, one of those small ones. This steaming hot piece of ass carried a damn *vibrator* with her. Man!

She put down her phone and started with the vibrator on her clit. I couldn't take it anymore. I put my phone down and start jerking myself off, watching her. We had to be very discreet, very quiet. There was no one around us, but the last thing we wanted was to draw any attention to ourselves.

This whole episode lasted maybe five minutes. Eight tops. I came all over the popcorn container next to me, and I could see her juice glistening between her legs. She gave me that sexy look again and smiled. She returned her vibrator to her purse and picked up her phone. She motioned for me to do the same.

Her: *Thank you.*

Thank you? She was thanking me?

Me: *You're welcome. Anytime.*

We sat through the rest of the movie, even the credits, without absorbing much of anything. We both waited until the lights came up before we moved. We adjusted our clothes and stood up slowly. Our kids were making their way up the steps to meet us. They loved the movie and asked us what we thought. We both said it was the best movie we had seen in a long, long time.

15

Grounding the Hog

CAN YOU LOVE YOUR wife but hate the sex? That's me. Can you love your husband but hate the sex? That's my friend Jen. So we help each other out. Know what I mean?

Jen and I are friends from years ago. We worked together and always had a connection. We tried dating, but the timing was off and it didn't work. We have stayed in touch through the years, through my marriage and kids and her marriage and kids. And of course we're also Facebook friends.

Things got interesting one night when Jen and I were Facebook chatting.

> Jen: *Ugh…I have to go now.*
> Me: *Why?*
> Jen: *Sex time. So not in the mood.*

Me: *I hear ya. Thank God for Grey's Anatomy. It's what's keeping my wife not looking at the clock and wondering why I'm not in bed yet.*

Jen: *How is it that for both of us? Two sexually driven people who don't want to get up there and get laid? What the fuck?*

Me: *It's not me for sure.*

Jen: *It's not me. . .4 SURE!*

Me: *I think it's what's waiting for us upstairs.*

Jen: *How did it even get to that point?*

Me: *Kids, life, work...*

Jen: *It's like fucking groundhog day in my bed. Same thing, over and over.*

Me: *No originality.*

Jen: *No oomph.*

We suddenly realize that we are both in the same exact, rickety sex boat.

Me: *I just had a wild idea.*

We were in the same boat. But what if we could be each other's life jackets?

Me: *I love my wife. You love your husband. Right?*

Jen: *Right.*

Me: *We're both not interested in going elsewhere for the lay.*

Jen: *Totally.*

Me: *Just stay with me on this thought. What if we help each other out? I'll scratch your back and you scratch mine.*

Jen: *Not following.*

Me: *Ever had phone sex?*

Jen: *Who hasn't?*

Me: *Think phone sex. What happens after you have it?*

Jen: *I'm incredibly turned on. I want it.*

Me: *Ok. So take phone sex and bring into the new century. Phone sex of 2010. . .ladies and gentlemen I'm talking Facebook sex. Or, in our case, Facebook Foreplay.*

Jen: *I'm listening.*

Me: *If we have Facebook sex on here and get each other incredibly aroused, when it's time to go up to the bedroom, we're just gonna wanna fuck our brains out. Follow me?*

Jen: *I follow.*

That night, we started our experiment. With the help of Facebook chat, we typed out our fantasies: my cock in her pussy; me fucking her brains out; her bent over a virtual kitchen counter. I think that last one did the trick. The next night, we meet up again on Facebook.

Me: *Well?*

Jen: *LOL! Well?*

Me: *I'm a fucking genius!*

Jen: *Yes you are.*

Me: *Details.*

Jen: *I was so fucking turned on by our chat that I just went up there and fucked him. We hadn't had sex like that in a long time.*

Me: *Ha-ha...same with me. We did it twice last night.*

Jen: *The orgasm was incredible.*

Me: *I'm glad. I do have one question though. When you had that incredible orgasm, who did you think of? Me or him?*

Jen: *Wouldn't you like to know. . .*

That was six months ago and the rest is history. Jen and I meet on Facebook twice a week for our foreplay...and I tell ya, it's the best fucking foreplay I've ever had.

16

Accidental Lesbian

IT TOTALLY HAPPENED BY accident. I swear! It was totally an accident. I would never tell anyone about it and I certainly would never, ever admit how glad I was that it happened. But, yeah, hell yeah I'm glad it happened. That's how good it was.

It was one of those late nights on Facebook. I had my glass of wine, my kids were fast asleep, and my husband was out playing poker. I was in bed, on my laptop, checking out who was online. A friend of mine—whose husband was playing poker with mine—was. I don't remember who popped who up, but we started chatting.

At first, there was nothing unusual about the conversation. After all, we'd chatted a ton of times before. . .about our husbands, our kids, our weekend plans. Why would this time be any different? Maybe it was the wine, maybe it was the full moon that was out, but this night, this night was very different.

It started with a simple, yet provocative question.

> Her: *Hey, Can I ask you something and you promise not to laugh?*
>
> Me: *Of course! You know you can ask me anything. . . LOL!*
>
> Her: *It's kind of embarrassing, but wtf. . .here it goes. Do you use a vibrator and if so, what kind?*

She was right! That was kind of embarrassing. My vibrator usage is not something I normally discuss with people other than my husband. Yet, here was my friend—my *good* friend—and she felt comfortable enough to ask me about this taboo topic, so I didn't want to leave her hanging.

> Me: *Lol! Umm. . ..yes I do use a vibrator. I actually have two.*
>
> Her: *Wow. . .you do? Two?*
>
> Me: *Yes. Don't you have one?*
>
> Her: *Lol! No, I don't. That's why I was asking. But I'm thinking of getting one. Or Two. . . lol!*
>
> Me: *So funny! You totally should get one. . .or two. It's a good thing, great thing actually.*
>
> Her: *Do you recommend the ones you have? What are they called?*
>
> Me: *Hang on. . .I'll get them and tell you more.*

I went into my closet and pulled my two vibrators out of my

hiding place.

> Me: *I have the pocket rocket. . .a great little toy. I also have the Rabbit.*
>
> Her: *What's the difference between the two?*
>
> Me: *Wow. . .you really don't know about this stuff, do you?*
>
> Her: *Nope. . .that's why I'm asking.*

It's a good thing I was feeling a little buzz with my wine. I don't know if I could have been so candid with her. This is not an everyday conversation for my friends and me. I took a deep breath, and typed on.

> Me: *Ok. The pocket rocket is small, and it's for clitoral stimulation. The rabbit looks like a dildo, like a penis, but it has dual stimulation. The penis part goes in and out of your vagina, while the top portion stimulates the clit. I know. . . a little graphic, but you asked.*
>
> Her: *Sounds pretty amazing. Which do you prefer?*
>
> Me: *They do different things. If I need a quickie, the pocket rocket usually does the trick. If I want to feel the sexual sensation, well, the rabbit is the one to go with. If you position it just the right way, it hits the g-spot and gets the clit going at the same time. It can get pretty intense.*
>
> Her: *That does sound intense.*
>
> Me: *It is. Whether I'm by myself or with Richard, it's*

great. I've even used it here before.

Her: *Here?!*

Me: *On Facebook. On chat. With Richard when he's out of town on business.*

Her: *I didn't even know things like that went on here.*

Me: *Of course shit like that happens. It's very hot. . . You're in your bed, on your laptop, wine by your side . . .it gets very hot. Haha. . .*

Her: *What's haha?*

Me: *The way I described it. It's exactly how I am now. In bed, on my laptop, wine by my side. . . except you're not Richard.*

Her: *And you're not getting hot. . .or are you. . . lol?*

What? Had she asked me if I was getting hot? Where the hell was this going? And suddenly, thinking about it, I realized, Yeah, I'm a little hot. Fuck!

Her: *U still there?*

Me: *Yeah, just thinking about what you just asked me.*

Her: *Look, I didn't mean to make you uncomfortable. It's just you're telling me about all this, and it's doing something to me. OMG, did I just type that?*

Me: *Yes, you did. And yes, if we are being that open here, then yes, it's making me hot.*

Her: *Should we do something about it?*

I wasn't sure what she was implying. I was planning on using my vibrator anyway tonight. Did she mean we should do something about it now, on Facebook? With each other? Gulp!

> Me: *You mean, the two of us?*
>
> Her: *Lol. Yeah, why the fuck not?*
>
> Me: *Ummm. . . .*
>
> Her: *Look, I have never ever done anything like this. We're talking about this shit, we both are feeling it. What's wrong with it? We have our husbands, our kids, but we only live once. Sometimes we just gotta say, what the fuck?*

OMG!

> Me: *Ok. You're right. It doesn't make us Lesbos. Just two drunk moms pleasuring our own bodies. Right?*
>
> Her: *Right. . . . So which one are you gonna use?*
>
> Me: *Pocket Rocket. But wait, you don't have anything.*
>
> Her: *I've used my fingers for this long. . .they'll do the trick.*
>
> Me: *Then let's do it. Do you wanna chat as we're doing it?*
>
> Her: *Yeah. . .we can one-hand type and tell each other what we're doing.*
>
> Me: *Vibrator is on. Let's do it.*
>
> Her: *I didn't realize how wet I was. Mmm. . .it feels good. What about you?*
>
> Me: *Feels damn good, I must say. Pretty wet over here,*

too.

Her: Mmmmm. . .I'm so turned on right now.

Me: Me 2. I'm naked. . .all naked. And the vibrator is right on my clit.

Her: I'm deep inside my vagina. In and out. . .so wet.

Me: What are you thinking about?

Her: I kind of wish you were here to see me in person.

Me: I never thought I would even say this, but me, too. My pussy is so wet.

Her: If I was there I would have my fingers in your wet pussy.

Me: And I would lick your pussy until you couldn't stand it anymore.

Who the fuck was I talking like this? It had to be the wine. . . damn good wine.

Her: OMG, I want you to lick my pussy so bad.

Me: I'm gonna come soon. OMG. . .it feels so fucking good.

Her: I want you to come.

Me: I'm gonna come. . .you too. . .u gotta come.

Her: If you come, I'll come.

Me: Ohhhhhh. . . .

Her: Ohhhh. . . .

And we came. Together. It took a few minutes for us both to recover. In fact, we both went idle on the chat screen.

Me: *That was. . .*

Her: *Pretty awesome.*

Me: *Incredible.*

Her: *Our little secret.*

Me: *Our little secret.*

Me: *So. . .*

Her: *What now?*

Me: *Don't know.*

Her: *Play it by ear?*

Me: *Sounds good to me.*

Play it by ear, she'd said. And so we did. . . every single Thursday night thereafter. When our guys were at poker.

Part Three

Back to Life,
Back to Reality

FOR THE MOST PART, what happens on Facebook can, and should, stay on Facebook. However, these online dalliances can start to encroach on your real life for any number of reasons. It can be tempting to think that something as fun as playful sex-chatting could easily translate into an in-person experience, but this is not always the case. On the plus side, if you suspect there might be a real romance brewing, the only way to find out is to meet the person face-to-face. On the minus side, real-life encounters with people from your past can stir up emotions that remained dormant while your interaction was online.

These are stories of people whose Facebook lives encroach on their real lives in unexpected ways. In one story, a married woman "switches teams"; in another, a divorced man suddenly sees an old friend in a totally different light.

17

I'm So Hard for You

I HAD ALREADY BEEN on Facebook for a while when I found Chris. We went to college together, lived in the same dormitory, and were always good friends. I'd always thought he was cute, and there was an attraction, but nothing had ever happened. As soon as I saw him on Facebook, I sent him a friend request. He replied right away and said he was very happy to have heard from me.

After a few back-and-forth emails, we started chatting. He lived on one coast, and I on the other. We were both married with kids and nearing forty. We would meet up to chat after he got home, late usually, from work, and everyone in my house was in bed.

As time progressed, so did our chats. What had begun as innocent conversations suddenly turned into deep discussions of what could have been and what could *still* be between the two of us.   We were both happily married, but we became outlets for one another. Nothing could ever come of it in real life, since we were both married and so far apart. So the fun really was harmless.

Chris would always tell me how attracted he was to me, how he felt when he thought of me, and what he would do to me if we were alone.

> Chris: *I would caress your whole body and touch you everywhere.*
> Chris: *I would take you from behind and grab onto your tits as I ride you.*
> Chris: *I can't wait to taste you.*

While my marriage was happy, my husband never talked to me like that. So there was something new and stimulating about it. I felt sexier with Chris talking (or shall I say typing) his sexy thoughts to me.

Did I reciprocate? Did I talk dirty to him as well? I guess I did (blush!), but I always thought he did a much better job at it. My sex talk usually consisted of a few "oh, yeah's" and an "I love it when you talk dirty to me" every once in a while. Regardless, Chris still popped me up. I guess, whatever I was doing, I was doing right.

This back and forth sex talk lasted several months, and it was inevitable that we'd want to take it further somehow. Why not talk on the phone? We wanted to hear each other's voices and do a whole lot more. Since we knew we were good at turning each other on through our words, it could only be better on the phone, right?

One Saturday when my husband was out with the kids, I logged onto Facebook. Chris was online as well, and his wife and kids were out of town. We figured it was the perfect (and rare) opportunity to do what we had been wanting to do.

I gave him my number; he called. I thought I was going to pick up the phone and we would just pick right up where we left off on Facebook. Boy, was I wrong! Talk about awkward. It just wasn't the same. I felt I was talking to a stranger, not the guy who had said all those intimate things to me on Facebook. I mean it had been almost twenty years since I had heard his voice!

The small talk went on for so long, I truly wasn't sure if I would be able to get down to the dirty deed. The whole thing was a lot different from what I'd expected. It was one thing to type that I wanted him, and another thing to say it out loud! By the time the conversation turned in the right direction, I had to convince myself to go through with it. This is what I wanted, right? Phone sex with this incredibly sexual and sensual guy. Of *course* I wanted that!

> Him: *What are you wearing?*
>
> Me: *A tank top and shorts. What are you wearing?*
>
> Him: *Boxers and a t-shirt. Mmmmm. I'm so hard for you. I'm stroking my cock. Where's your hand?*
>
> Me: *Where do you want it to be?*
>
> Him: *I want you to feel your wet pussy.*
>
> Me: *I'm feeling—*

Uh, oh! The dog is barking, and there's noise downstairs. My husband and kids had gotten home early. I told Chris, and he hung up before I could say another word.

After that episode, things were never the same. I think my family interrupting brought him back to reality. We no longer have our long chats, and when we are online at the same time we don't pop each other up.

What happened? I think when you chat on Facebook, you have no inhibitions. You are typing, not talking. You get away with a lot more. You say more things than you would not say in person or on the phone. It made me realize that chatting on Facebook won't always translate to another medium. Facebook is its own special thing.

Chris and I were good friends, and now we hardly talk. Do I wish we hadn't taken that next step? No, because I would always have been curious had we not. It was a lesson for me: What happens on Facebook really should stay on Facebook.

18

He Loves Me,
She Loves Me Not

Travis and I dated briefly in high school. It truly wasn't a healthy relationship. I wanted to take care of him, since he was in a really bad place at the time. He was not getting along with his parents and had no one to turn to. I wanted to be the one to make him all better, to fix him. The problem was, only he was able to fix himself, which he didn't want to do, and soon enough, I ended our relationship.

This unhealthy connection didn't cease on the best of terms. He blamed me, was angry with me, pointed the finger at me—the usual co-dependent, unhealthy thing one does. In time, his anger, and our communication, faded. I went on with my life, as did he.

Thirty years have passed, and we are now adults. As everyone else has, I've jumped on the Facebook bandwagon, and one day I noticed that Travis had joined Facebook. I contemplated whether

I should friend him. I knew, eventually, he would see me on there, since we did have friends in common.

I decided to bite the bullet and friend him. There was a lot of back-and-forth before I let him back in my life. Was he married? Divorced. Did he have kids? One. Was he close with his family? Yes. Was he working? Yes. After feeling he was in a much better and healthier place than he had once been, I began a Facebook friendship with him.

At the same time as our renewed friendship was budding, I was having unhappy feelings in my own marriage. I was not attracted to Travis at all, but I looked forward to chatting with him on Facebook. We talked about the past, the future, and our lives. In a way, I was still nurturing him and helping him by giving him advice on everything from dating girls to changing careers. Once again, a co-dependent friendship sprouted between us.

One day, Travis emailed me that we should meet for coffee. I didn't see any harm, so I did. I didn't tell anyone what I was doing because I knew my friends would kill me. They knew about my past with Travis and would have told me there is no reason for us to meet.

As I pulled up, a part of me felt uncomfortable I was about to meet him, and that no one would know where I was or whom I was with. So as I sat in the car, I left a note next to my seat—that I was meeting Travis for coffee on this date and time, in case anything were to happen to me. I knew he wasn't violent or capable of hurting me; something in my heart made me write it. It'd been over thirty years since I saw him face to face, and I just had to do it.

I walked into the coffee shop first; he wasn't there yet. I looked around, took a few deep breaths and then saw him as he approached the door. He looked the same, a little older but not so much wiser. He had a small bouquet of flowers in his hand, which he gave to me. I instantly felt uncomfortable. I knew it was a nice, considerate gesture on his part, but I wasn't quite sure how he had interpreted our meeting. For me, it was just a quick coffee with an old friend—and, right away, I knew I had made a mistake.

At that moment, I realized that meeting someone and talking to someone on Facebook were two totally different things. When I'm sitting in the security and comfort of my own home typing away at my keyboard, I am safe. I can say and do what I want, and it's not so intimate. Out in the world, in the open, face to face, it's real: It's not as safe, and the boundaries have changed. Seeing him again, in the flesh, brought back weird feelings and reminded me why I didn't want him in my life.

He didn't do anything wrong. Maybe the flower thing threw me off. In fact, he was very, very nice. I just couldn't deal with it. The bad memories resurfaced. The history between us was way too much for me to handle, especially with all the other drama in my life.

He bought me a coffee, and we sat outside and talked. I kept checking my watch, knew I couldn't be rude, yet I wanted to get back to my car, to my home. After about twenty minutes, I told him I had to leave. He respected that, and we went our separate ways.

The moment I got back in my car, I tore up the note, realizing that, even in writing it, I had known in my heart it was wrong to meet and be friends with this person.

As soon as I got home, I threw the flowers in my neighbor's outside garbage can. The last thing I needed was for my husband to ask where I'd gotten them.

As I entered my house, my cell phone rang. The caller ID said *Travis*. I let it go to voicemail.

I went into my office and logged onto Facebook. There was a message in my inbox from him. This had to end, I told myself. Now. So I sent him a note.

> *Thank you again for the coffee and flowers. I appreciate your friendship, but right now things are a little crazy in my life. I hope you understand. I wish you the best of luck with everything.*

That was three months ago. Do I still hear from him? Occasionally. He still sends me a note, pops me up, or writes a comment on my wall—not a lot, but it happens every now and then. I know I could have defriended him, deleted him as a friend, but I didn't want to. I just felt it was okay to still have him as a Facebook friend.

Do I regret friending Travis in the first place? Yes and no. Yes because I really didn't need to bring him back into my life. We should just have stayed Facebook friends, not become friend friends. And no because I think I needed to learn a lesson.

Learn the lesson of the boundaries of Facebook, too: How you feel on a computer screen may not necessarily translate into real life.   I believe I needed this life lesson so now, as I continue Facebooking, I am careful with the friendships I pursue and create. Life is full of learning lessons, both good and bad, and this is one I needed to just experience for myself.

19

Li(c)king Pussy

WHEN I LOOK BACK now, I totally knew it in high school. I liked pussy. Not that I had a chance to like it, or lick it for that matter, but I definitely was curious about it.

I played the role. I dated the guy I was supposed to date. All the while I was eyeing the girls who were my friends. I pretended to like the guy, to like the cock, but in reality, all I really wanted was the vagina.

I went off to college and met my future husband right away. He was safe, a nice guy. We had a good relationship, and he was my best friend. We married soon after graduating college and had three children a few years later. Our marriage was fine.

"Fine" is the perfect word to describe it. He was good to me and provided for our family. I should have been doing fucking cartwheels to have a guy like him. But I wasn't.

I never hid the fact that I liked pussy. I would make comments to my husband all the time about other women. He knew I had a curiosity, but I don't think he ever took me seriously.

One night we were at a party at a friend's house. I was in the bathroom when a woman I knew as an acquaintance, a friend of a friend, accidently walked in on me. She apologized and started to turn; I said it was okay, she could stay. Well, one thing led to another, and we ended up kissing. She was not a lesbian by any means—in fact, her husband was also at the party. She was a mom of two with one too many margaritas in her, and when we kissed, it sealed the deal. I knew for sure I liked pussy.

I went home that night and touched myself while thinking of her. It wasn't even really *her* who turned me on, but the thought of being with another woman. I knew I had found my calling, and I needed more.

The next day, I told my husband what had happened. He was turned on when I told him (so typical for a man). He pretty much shrugged it off. I don't think he was too concerned that I would ever switch teams on him.

The curiosity lingered, though. It didn't go away. It consumed me. I was a faithful wife, but all I could think about was pussy. I knew I had to do something about this, so, on my own, I decided to take matters into my own hands.

I was already active on Facebook, and I thought I would peruse the lesbian groups to see if anyone piqued my interest. There were all types of girls on these groups, and I had no idea how many different types of lesbians existed. As far as I was concerned, all I wanted was vagina.

I started to look through the different pictures of the people in the group one by one, until I saw Shawna. She had red hair and blue eyes, and she just looked so happy in her picture. That's what pulled me to her, how happy she looked.

I sent her a message introducing myself. I had no idea if she was single or taken, where she lived, or even if she was interested in being my friend. It didn't take long for her to write me back. She was very sweet, and we became Facebook friends.

We struck up a great Facebook friendship. We'd chat every chance we got. I had totally lucked out, and she lived in my city. She was a few years older than me and a full-blown lesbian. I was honest with her about my situation; she didn't seem to mind that I was married with kids and trying to find myself sexually. In fact, I think she kind of liked that. I was fresh meat.

After about two weeks of Facebook chatting every day, we decided to meet and have a "date." I don't remember the last time I had been that nervous. I went out, bought a cute top to wear with my jeans, and even took the time to get a pedicure. I told my husband I was going out for a Mom's Night Out and went on my merry way to see Shawna.

We met at an Italian restaurant known for its ambiance and amazing Chianti. I walked in and there she was—it was hard not to miss her. She looked so hot sitting in the back corner booth waiting for me. When I approached, she rose, greeted me with a hug, and as the saying goes, she had me at hello.

We spent three hours in our corner booth at that little restaurant. We ordered two bottles of wine and devoured our pasta. We talked and laughed and shared our lives. As the night wore on, we sat closer and closer to each other, and our legs touched. She was very touchy-feely, and as she told stories she touched my arm or hand, and every time she did I tingled. I knew she would be my first girl.

After we shut the restaurant down, she asked me if I wanted to go back to her place. Of course I did! I followed her in my car, and as I drove, I put down all the windows, cranked up the radio, and sang my heart out. I haven't felt that alive in years.

By the time we got back to her house, I had made up my mind that I wanted to get in her pants as soon as possible. I think she was feeling the same way. She poured us some more wine, we sat on the couch, and she went in for a kiss. I could not get enough of her. When she kissed me, it was so soft, so warm, and felt so damn good.

She kissed me for a long time and worked her way down my neck. I moaned over and over. She took my shirt off and un-hooked my bra. She took my breast in her mouth and sucked me. She was in total control, and I loved it. I wanted her to do what-ever she wanted with me.

She took of my pants, and I let them fall down to the ground. When she slid down my panties, I could feel how wet I was. She put her fingers between my legs and put them inside me. She knew where to touch me, in all the right places, and it had never felt that good. I came right away, and then she moved down slowly until she started licking my pussy.

I tell you, there is nothing in the world that can compare to a woman going down on you. They totally know what the fuck they are doing—so much more than a man. She licked my clit until I couldn't stand it anymore. I came again and again and again.

At that point, all I wanted to do was to taste her, so I took her in my mouth. I had never tasted pussy, and hers was so sweet, so delicious, I couldn't get enough of her. We moved to a 69 and both licked each other over and over, harder and deeper. Man, I was thinking, have I died and gone to heaven?

After what seemed like hours of going down on each other, she turned us around and our pussies started to kiss. We ground each other harder and harder. I have never come so much without using a vibrator. She took me to places I had never been before. I knew I was home.

I spent that night at Shawna's. All night long we talked, kissed, explored, and fucked. It was the perfect night.

The next morning, when I came home, the kids were already off to school. I took a long, hot shower and had to figure out what I was going to tell my husband. I knew it was not a phase or something I had to get out my system. It was me, the new me, and this new me liked pussy—loved it.

20

Touchdown

IT'S BEEN ABOUT SIX months, give or take, since my divorce. I was a good husband. . .not great, good. I definitely could have been better. I was a pretty good dad. . .not fabulous, but pretty good. I worked, brought home the bacon, and did what I was supposed to do. My ex-wife is a good woman, but we never fit. You know the talk about couples being two pieces of a puzzle that fit; well, that wasn't us. We liked each other—heck, we loved each other. We just were never in love.

I ran into a buddy of mine from college a few months back who asked me if I was on Facebook. I knew about it but had never signed up. I couldn't believe how many fraternity brothers he kept in touch with. . .all from this Facebook thing. I decided that, the following weekend, when I didn't have my kids, I would check this thing out.

Within hours of logging on, I was already up to thirty-eight friends. I couldn't believe the people who'd found me and the people I'd found. It'd been a little over twenty years since I graduated high school, so some of these people looked the same while others looked a hell of a lot different. The guys were losing their hair (I'm still lucky in that department), and the women were lookin' good. Many of them were married, with kids, some are divorced, like me—and some have never been to the altar.

A few weeks after I joined, I came home one night and found a friend request from a friend of the past. Ben and I had grown up together, played little league, ridden our bikes around town, and been teammates on our high school football team. He was a good guy, a good friend. I couldn't pinpoint when we had lost touch—we just had. I'd gone back East to college, and he'd stayed in town. Anyway, Ben friended me, and of course I accepted his friend request.

The next day I found a message in my Inbox:

> *Hey Tom. It's Ben, buddy! How the hell are ya? Great to see you on this crazy thing we call Facebook (or when it's acting up, Assbook). Would love to catch up with you, grab a drink. Give me a call.*

I did, and we decided to meet at a local sports bar for a drink and watch the game. We had a great time. The moment we spotted each other, it was like back in school. We laughed, reminisced about the days of playing football, and caught up.

After that night, Ben and I started hanging out more and

more. We caught a baseball game, went to the movies, attended a concert or two. Ben had never married, never had kids. He was the ultimate bachelor and, on my free weekends, I was, too. When we weren't hanging out, we would hang out on Facebook, chat, share funny "fail posters," find friends from the past.

As time passed, Ben became a fixture in my life, an important friend and confidante. I trusted him, believed in him, and enjoyed our friendship. His parents were thrilled to see me back in their lives, and there was many a Sunday night that I joined them all for a home-cooked meal. For the first time, in a long time, I felt good.

Christmas came. My ex took the kids to visit her family back East, and I was alone. I had gotten a few amazing bottles of wine as a gift from a client. Ben called to see what I was up to, and I told him I was just about to pop open a bottle. When I invited him to join me, he was eager to come over and sample the goods.

With wine in hand and the basketball game humming in the background, Ben and I settled down on my couch. We were soon almost done with bottle number two, and for some reason we kept moving a little closer to each other. We were talking, turning our heads a few times to look at the television, but always turning back towards each other. We were both wasted, buzzed beyond belief, but not to the point that we both didn't know what was happening.

I don't know who started it. I think it was a mutual thing. I don't know why at that point it happened. All I know is. . .it did.

We kissed. And we kissed. And we kissed. I have never kissed a man, never thought about wanting to. A part of me was grossed out, but another incredibly intrigued. I let Ben kiss me, and I kissed him back. What the fuck? If this experience was going to happen, no better person than my childhood best friend.

Our kissing lasted for a long time and then he went down on me. The rest was history. That whole night was one for the books.

Ben spent the night, and the next morning, when I woke up, he was gone. I sat in bed, rubbing my eyes, not sure if the things I was remembering were real or a dream. I wasn't sure how to feel. Had I enjoyed it? Was I grossed out? Was I good? Was I bad? Did this ruin our friendship? Strengthen it? I know I'm not gay, at least I don't think so, but then why had I done what I did last night? So many questions were running through my head, I didn't know what the hell to think. And where the hell was Ben? Had he crawled away in shame? Did he think I initiated it? I know I hadn't. We both had. Was he disgusted? I knew it was fucking awkward—but it was even more fucked up that he wasn't there to figure out this shit with me.

I jumped in the shower and just didn't know what to think. Ben is a great guy, a great friend. I didn't want to lose the friendship that I'd just rediscovered. Yet, at the same time, I wasn't sure in which direction I wanted to take it. What the fuck!

I hopped out the shower and got dressed. All the while my head was spinning and spinning.

Then my doorbell rang. It was Ben, with a shit-eating grin and holding two cups of coffee. I tell ya, it's going to be one hell of an interesting morning.

21

Stalkerazzi

WHEN IT COMES TO Facebook, you control it all: Who writes on your wall, what people can see, what pictures they can view. You can friend a person and give them complete access to your life, or you can limit every single item on your wall. You are in the driver's seat, and your friends are your passengers.

I am the driver of my Facebook page. Sometimes I'm driving at full speed, changing my status daily, posting pictures and sharing You Tube music clips. Yet, sometimes, I'm going at cruise control. . .changing my status every few days, posting a picture every now and then. My mood at home will determine my Facebook mood.

I love when people comment on my statuses. I love to hear what they have to say and what they want to share. But sometimes it can go too far.

I have a boyfriend—a great, fabulous guy. We went to high school together, and we are now at the adult phase in our life and have reconnected through Facebook. We have both been married, divorced, and have a few kids between us. We love each other with all our hearts, and we hope this relationship will lead to a lifetime together. In the meantime, we have Facebook.

We are both very active Facebook users. We comment on each other's posts and statuses daily. We will post a status, sometimes, that only we will understand. Facebook is just another way we communicate in our relationship—a fun way of communication . . .until it leads to feelings of hurt, jealousy, and anger.

When we first started our relationship, we were very private about it. We didn't change our relationship status on Facebook to announce that we were now in a relationship with another. Our close friends knew something was happening between us. . . that was fine, and we were happy to share it with them. The Facebook lurkers, who were able to catch wind of it that, bothered us the most, especially when lurkers are ex-boyfriends who also went to high school with us, and who still had a thing for the girl that dumped them twenty years ago. That girl being me.

The first time it happened, we wrote it off as a fluke, but then it started happening again and again and again. Every time my boyfriend would comment on my status, the ex would, of course, also make a statement. And many times when I commented on my boyfriend's posts on his wall, the ex would make a statement as well.

The ex's comments started off as funny but then took a personal turn. Here and there he would make a snide comment, an off-the-mark sexual observation, very subtle, but there—suggesting something was happening between me and my boyfriend. Once he remarked about how "well" he knew me.

My boyfriend and I jokingly referred to him as my *stalkerazzo*, and although we joked we knew it was no longer funny. This ex-boyfriend was getting a thrill out of our relationship. It wasn't dangerous by any means, but he wanted to push buttons. He wanted to get that rise. And it was working.

I asked another friend of mine for advice. What would he do? Incredibly, they too were dealing with a Facebook *stalkerazzo*. The situation was different, but stalking was also involved.

My friend has a Facebook friend who is a girl. Any time he posts a photo (not of himself, but of funny things he finds) or a music video, this girl pulls a Facebook front and swipes his goods. She takes his photo and posts it, on her wall, as hers. Sometimes she gives credit where credit is due, but most of the time she just posts his stuff. She has also been known to steal his status.

His take on it: She was lonely. She didn't have anything better to do, and he felt that defriending her would just cause more harm than good.

I told this story to my boyfriend, and we too discussed our options. Do we defriend? Do we block him? What to do? In the end, we decided to ignore him. Sometimes the best way to deal with a situation is not to deal. If we drew attention to him, he'd continue. If we blocked or defriended him, it could cause unforeseen problems. So we ignored. And we ignored and we ignored.

And finally, finally, the comments stopped. Maybe he moved

onto another ex-girlfriend. . .or maybe, just maybe, I should do a Facebook hookup and introduce him to my *friend's* stalker. That could end up being a match made in stalker heaven!

22

Where I Want to Be

I AM MARRIED, with three kids, and love, love, *love* going on Facebook. I don't know what it is—maybe an escape from reality—but it's something I do on a daily basis.

Robert and I are friends on Facebook. . .well, more than friends. We dated in high school. It was totally innocent. We were young, and that was a different time. We fooled around a lot but never did the deed, never went all the way. I have to admit, though, I had always been very curious about him.

Robert is married, too. He has two kids and lives in another state. We have enjoyed our friendship on Facebook, reconnecting and, as well, doing some major flirting.

Before I knew it, Robert was all I was thinking about. When I was in line at carpool picking up the kids, in the shower, even when my husband and I were making love, it was Robert's face in my mind. I knew he was feeling something for me, too.

One day he emailed me on Facebook that he was coming into town for a business meeting. We talked about it and arranged to meet.

It was a Tuesday, and I had some free time. I dropped the kids off at school and met Robert at his hotel. I wasn't sure what would happen, but I did know I was open to anything. I know, I know. . .I'm married. Right now I have no intention of leaving my husband, but there's something about Robert that I can't get out of my mind. I had to know if this was only a virtual feeling or if seeing him in real life would make a difference.

I will never forget the moment he opened the door to his hotel room. All we had to do was take one look at each other's eyes, and we were lost. It was an amazing day of talking, cuddling, kissing, and making love. I was totally in the moment, as was he, and not once did I stop to think about my kids, my husband, or what I was doing. I had no guilt, only pleasure. It was just like I'd thought it would be. We felt as if we were back in high school, but it was so much better! The sex was intense, and I have never felt so incredible. Just thinking about it brings shivers to my body.

Of course, all good things come to an end. That day went by quickly, and I needed to go back to "reality" and get home to make dinner. We promised to chat on Facebook later on, and as soon as I put my kids to bed, we did so through the night.

Robert went back home the next day. We still talk just as much as we used to, and he sends me little texts when it's "safe." We both have no regrets and know we have something there. He's trying to plan another business trip out here, and this time I will tell my husband that I'm going away to a spa for the night. I can't wait to spend the night with Robert and wake up in his arms. Mmm. . . cannot wait!

I wasn't sure what would happen when we mixed fantasy with reality, but for us it worked and it was incredible. Look, I don't know what our future holds and what's going to happen, but I do know, for right now, this is where I want to be.

23

Viva Las Vegas

THE OTHER MORNING I woke up to a message in my Facebook Inbox:

> *I'll make your wishes come true. . .want to fly to Vegas on Friday?*

It had been sent at 3:12 a.m. At the time, my Facebook status had said something about how my wish bracelet had finally fallen off, and I'd asked, "When do my wishes start coming true?" This was a private response I'd gotten from Steve.

Steve, a college friend and married, was in Vegas on business. I knew this because his status updates were bragging to that effect.

We had done some harmless flirting over the previous few months, but inviting me to Vegas was moving our friendship to a whole new level.

For a moment, yes, it crossed my mind. What if I did go? What if I hopped on a plane and met him in Vegas for the night? Our little Facebook flirtations would become reality, and, as we all know, what happens in Vegas, stays in Vegas. We'd probably have insane sex and then we would both go back to our separate lives and remain friends. . .Facebook friends. So, yes, I admit, I thought about it. . .but only for a minute.

And then I came back to reality. Look at the time of that email. . .3:12 a.m. That's a fucking drunk Facebook email! One does not send sober emails at 3:12 a.m.!

So I thought about it once again and tried to decide how to handle it. Had he regretted hitting the send button right after he sent it—or, even in his presumably drunken state, known what he was doing and wanted me out there? I also knew your true feelings are supposed to come out when you're drunk, so maybe he really did have feelings for me. . .married or not.

So I waited. I gave it some time. . .maybe an hour. . .to see if he would write me again with an *OMG, I sent you an email last night when I was totally wasted and don't even know what I wrote,* but I didn't get that. I didn't get anything. So I played it safe. I decided to write back:

> *Looking at the time u sent this email, 3:12 a.m., u were probably wasted! Ha! Not sure what state of mind u were in when u sent this.*

I waited again for a response. And waited. And waited. And

waited. Never heard back from him. Was he mortified? Embarrassed? Mad? Angry?

Several days later, when I logged onto Facebook, what I saw had me laughing so hard I nearly fell out of my bed. There, on the Highlights section of Facebook, were various pictures of my Facebook friends. One in particular caught my eye. It was of Steve and his wife. I clicked on it and there they were. . . together . . .in Vegas! She'd been with him in Vegas when he was emailing me to fly out and rendezvous with him. What the fuck had he been thinking?

I never hear from Steve again; I guess the Vegas email will always be a mystery. Had he been that drunk? Where was his wife? Did he want to put me up in the hotel so he could escape her and be with me? I may never know, but as I said, I guess it's true that whatever happens in Vegas stays in Vegas.

24

Shut Up and Do Me

IS YOUR PUSSY WET YET?

That's my husband for you. Away on business, logged onto Facebook—and that's the message he leaves in my Inbox, my cue that he wants to have Facebook sex.

It wasn't always like this. Our sex life was dull, incredibly bland, and very missionary, nothing to write home about, very *Groundhog Day*. There was a time in our marriage that we didn't know if it would last. We had hit a huge bump, but we'd wanted to make it work. So we had tried and we did. This is part of the work—making our sex life fun, adventurous and different, very *un*missionary.

I get the kids to bed, get into my own, and log onto Facebook on my laptop: time for my husband to Facebook-fuck me.

It was Facebook that nearly broke up our marriage. The irony is that it is also what we hope is going to save it. That huge bump that we hit. . .for both of us. . .was a Facebook affair. It never crossed the line to reality, but both of us were having intimate Facebook conversations with someone other than ourselves. We could have gone on doing our own thing, but we are so in tune with each other that we knew something was up. After months of discussions and counseling, we realized we wanted to save our marriage and make an attempt to make it a great one. If Facebook sex worked for both of us with others, why couldn't it work for *us*. . .as a couple.

So, here he is, my husband, ready and waiting for my pussy to be wet.

I get into bed, wearing nothing. My laptop is poised, glass of wine beside me, and my Rabbit has brand-new batteries. I see him on chat and tell him I'm here and ready. I get out my lube and away we go.

> Husband: *Hey, honey, before we start, can you bring my gray shirt to the cleaners?*
>
> Wife: *Already did it and picked up your suit for the party this weekend.*
>
> Husband: *Ahhh. . .forgot we had that. You gonna wear your sexy black dress with those come fuck-me shoes . . .I love those.*
>
> Wife: *The Alaia ones. . .they are hot.*
>
> Husband: *I love when you wear them when I fuck you.*
>
> Wife: *Or should I wear the other dress. . .you know the one that's off the shoulder. . .then I would need to*

wear my Louboutin's. . .hmmm. . .I just don't—

Husband: *Honey. . .just shut up and fuck me.*

Wife: *Someone's ready. . .lol!*

Husband: *I want to put my hard cock in you.*

Wife: *Oh, baby, I want you in me.*

Husband: *I want you take your fingers and put them in your wet pussy.*

Wife: *Oohh, baby. . .I'm so wet.*

Husband: *Fuck yourself, baby. . .with your hands. Now spread those lips of yours so I can get my face in your pussy. You know you want me to lick you, don't you?*

Wife: *I love when you lick me. . .*

Husband: *Can you feel me. . .my magic tongue. . . inside your wet pussy licking you?*

Wife: *I feel it. . .I want your cock in me.*

Husband: *Not yet. . .I want to eat you dry. Lick you all up. Taste you. Smell you.*

Wife: *Fuck, you're amazing.*

Husband: *I want you to come. I want you to come all over my face.*

Wife: *I wanna come all over you. . .*

Husband: *I want you to come all over my face and then kiss me so you can taste yourself. . .how sweet you taste.*

Wife: *Ahh. . .I'm gonna come! Ahh—*

Silence ensues for a minute.

Wife: *Wow—*

Husband: *Shh—we're not done yet. Only just begun. Now take your rabbit and put it inside your wet pussy, in and out, in and out.*

Wife: *It feels so fucking good. . .your cock in me. Harder, baby. Harder.*

Husband: *Harder and faster. I'm fucking you. I love to fuck you.*

Wife: *I love watching you going in and out. In and out.*

Husband: *You are all mine and I love it. I love to feel your wet pussy with my hard cock.*

Wife: *Fuck, baby. . .you have a way with words.*

Husband: *I have a way with a lot of things. . .*

Wife: *Oh, yes, you do. . .I love what you do with your cock.*

Husband: *Yeah?*

Wife: *I love how hard it is inside of me. Fuck me more.*

Husband: *Fuck!*

Wife: *Fuck!*

Husband: *Did you finish?*

Wife: *About three times. . .shit!*

Husband: *What? Three times is not enough?*

Wife: *No. . .the baby's crying. Fuck! Gotta run.*

Husband: *Ha-ha. . .always the baby.*

Wife: *Thanks, honey. . .you rock my world.*

And so we get off—excuse the pun—and go back to life, back to reality.

Part Four

You Can't Always
Get What You Want

HERE'S THE DOWNSIDE OF Facebook: It's pretty public. Sure you can tinker with your privacy settings or use a phony name, but the chances are good that someone who you didn't intend to—your spouse, your son, your boss—may see your page, posts, friends, etc. And even if you didn't do anything wrong, a spouse who uncovers a secret of yours on Facebook is liable to be pretty upset.

These are stories about rage, mostly righteous—from the man who is happy to catch his wife in a Facebook affair, to the man who discovers the same and is incensed. While romance can be an incendiary event, Facebook only fans the flames.

25

Getting Caught

IT WAS SO FUCKING INNOCENT. That's what pisses me off the
most—so damn innocent, and it gets blown up like this. The way
my husband is reacting, I might as well have gotten laid out of it.
I might as well have had someone go down on me, fuck me, and
make me come like there was no tomorrow, because I am feeling
so fucked right now, it might as well have felt good.

This is what happened. I'm Facebook friends with my ex-
boyfriend. The guy that was my first love, my first fuck. We're
talking high school love, the one I said I would marry, but I was
a fucking teenager, for God's sake!

I met my husband right out of college, and he always had a
thing against this guy—let's call him Mr. X.

Mr. X. and I always stayed friends through the years, yet my
husband didn't want me to have a friendship with him or have

him as a part of our lives. My husband meant the world to me, so I respected his wishes, and Mr. X. and I went our separate ways.

Flash forward to years later. I'm talking time has passed; children are no longer babies years later. We're now in our late thirties...that's how many years later it is. Well, Mr. X. and I become Facebook friends. The hubby knows, not thrilled with it, but what could he do?

One night, a late night, Mr. X. and I were both online at the same time. We started chatting and realized it'd been about ten years since we last saw each other. We had run into each other, with our families, at a party and exchanged cordial hellos. We couldn't even count that as seeing each other. We truly couldn't remember the last time we'd actually sat down and caught up. He asked if I wanted to meet for lunch. What the hell, I thought. I said yes.

I decided not to tell my husband. I wasn't cheating on him. I wasn't planning on having an affair, but I knew that, if my husband found out that I was going to meet Mr. X., the shit would hit the fan. I wasn't in the mood to deal with my husband about anything, especially that. The meeting was purely platonic, purely a catch-up lunch, and I knew my husband would forbid it. So I said fuck it and I met Mr. X.

As I drove out to the restaurant, I was second-guessing my decision—not about the meeting but about hiding it from my husband. Should I just tell him I'd run into the guy at Starbucks? Should I lie and say I'd seen him, but under different circumstances?

No, this meeting was for me. I didn't need to report anything to my husband. I was a big girl, and I could make big-girl decisions. This was one of them.

When I walked into the dark restaurant, there he was in a corner booth. He had aged well and still had that sexy smile he'd always had. We sat down and talked, non-stop, for two hours. We forgot to even order lunch. . .just had drinks. We laughed, caught up, remembered, and reminisced. We played the "Where's so-and-so" and "What's so-and-so doing now" game. We flirted a little, but nothing over the edge, nothing that would suggest to anyone else that there was an attraction there.

Don't get me wrong. I know we were both still attracted to each other, but we were both totally off limits. We were married, parents and in committed relationships, yet there is no harm in a little flirt and a little discussion of what it could be like if we did end up in bed together. Not that we wanted that, but just the thought of how more experienced we were. . . there was no harm in saying how awesome the sex between us would be today. . .was there?

Two hours and a glass and a half of wine later, we both had to call it a day. He had to go back to work, and I had to go back to mom duties and pick up the kids from school. We hugged goodbye, and that was that. No kiss, no caress, no booty call. The bell had rung, and lunchtime was over.

That afternoon I was busy being soccer mom to the kids, picking them up, running the carpool, getting materials for a science project, doing homework—the usual mom duties. I didn't have a chance to check into Facebook or look at my emails. . . until the phone rang.

My husband was on the other line and he did not seem happy. I was preoccupied with the kids and couldn't really talk and told him so. He said he had one thing to ask me: "Did you see Mr. X?" My heart skipped a beat. "Just tell me the truth. Did you see Mr. X?"

I didn't know what to say. I don't know how. But he knew where I was today. Motherfucker. "Yes, but—"

"We will discuss this when I get home. I don't even know what to say to you right now. At least you told me the truth."

And he hung up.

I was shocked. Had someone seen me? Had my husband *followed* me? How the hell did he know? I couldn't concentrate. I couldn't see straight, but I had to be Mom and push the issue aside for the time being.

I had dinner made and on the table. I had a few minutes, so I checked my email. I knew it would be a long night with my husband and I wouldn't have time to do it later. I logged onto my account and noticed I had several emails. All were bold, all were unread, except one—marked as read and from Facebook. A damn Facebook notification telling me someone had emailed me on Facebook, a fucking news bulletin that told me, *Hey, dumb shit, check your inbox for a message from Mr. X.*

My husband came home, and we sat as a family for dinner. There was plenty of tension, but we didn't let the kids know. I got them showered and ready for bed, taking my time, knowing what was waiting for me downstairs.

He was sitting in the den with his evening drink in hand, calm, reserved. His face didn't reveal a thing. I listened as he told me what had happened that afternoon. He'd been looking for an email from someone, couldn't find it on his account, thought maybe it was on mine. He knows my password. Why the hell not? I have nothing to hide. . .at least I used to have nothing to hide.

As he looked for the email, he happened to see Mr. X's name in my inbox. The name was listed under the Facebook notification. My husband had clicked on the email and read the notification. All the email contained was a note telling me to have a nice afternoon—totally innocent, one friend to another.

My husband did not go on my Facebook account. Seeing an interaction with Mr. X was enough. He didn't know we'd seen each other. He just assumed it and straight out asked me. I'd blown my cover without even having to. I could have just said that we had exchanged a few emails on Facebook. My husband had no proof that we had met.

My husband was livid. He reminded me how sensitive he was to my relationship with Mr. X—the one person, the one damn person in the world that he didn't want me to interact with, and here I was doing just that. "Just tell me why. Why do you have a need to see him? There had to be a reason you had this need."

Honestly, there was none. I mean, I guess there was a curiosity. Yes, for sure there was a curiosity. But that's it, nothing more, nothing less. My husband would not accept this, and now our marriage is on the line. This innocent lunch has turned into making marriage-counselor appointments and questions about whether he can ever trust me again.

I have a long fucking road ahead of me dealing with this bullshit and smoothing everything out. The one thing I did do, as soon as I could, was change my Facebook settings. I will no longer *ever* get an email notifying of me of anything on Facebook. He will never stumble upon another Facebook email again. I always knew that, if I Facebook chatted with someone I had the CCH option (Clear Chat History), which I do often, but I had never been warned, or ever thought, about the email notifications. Now I know. . . .

In the meantime, I am fucked. My marriage is fucked, and all for nothing. I never even talked to Mr. X again. I mean, we are Facebook friends, but we never reconnected again. A simple, innocent lunch may end up changing my life. So, yes, if I knew this was gonna happen anyway, I should have just gotten fucked. And it would have been awesome.

26

Motherfucker

IT BEGAN SIX YEARS ago, before there was Facebook.

I was newly divorced, and he was married. Our kids went to preschool together, and we were at the obligatory birthday party. I'll always remember that day, looking at him from across the room, and thinking, What a hottie! He was exactly the kind of guy I would want, and the exact opposite of my ex.

I was the mom, he was the dad, and of course we exchanged the usual pleasantries: how nice the party was, how much fun the kids were having, and how fast time flew now that our kids were going off to kindergarten. We would be at one school, and they would be at another, so I knew my contact with this babe of a married dad would be limited.

I have to say, and I'm not just saying this or imagining it, there was an attraction there when we talked. I don't know what it was, but for sure there was a smidgen of flirtatiousness in our conversation. We parted ways, and Mr. Hottness stayed in the back of my mind and his image would become most useful in some of my moments of individual pleasure.

Six years later, I was out hiking with my girlfriend when she told me she had some gossip for me. "Remember Alex? That hottie dad from preschool?" How could I forget? He was a close friend of my vagina and vibrator. "Alex and his wife separated. Can you believe it?"

OMG, I thought. The hottie is available and single. I had not seen him in six years, but he had to still look the way he had when I last saw him. I had to get in touch with him.

That night, I went on Facebook and typed in his name. Yup, there he was, and his profile pic was a hot one. I sent him off a note, just saying hi, that it was good to see him on Facebook. One day passed, two pass, three, without a response. I asked my friend again whether it was true about his marital status. She confirmed it.

Four, five, six days went by, then a full week. This guy must either not be interested in getting back to me, I thought, or maybe he's not an active Facebook member.

Finally, on Day 10 I got the response I'd been waiting for! He apologized for not getting back to me sooner, but he'd been out of town and hadn't checked his Facebook page.

After some back and forth exchanges, we got down to the important stuff. He casually asked if I had anyone special in my life. I said I didn't. When I asked him how his wife was, he said they were separated.

I'm so sorry to hear that, I typed. Yeah, right. . .best fucking news I'd gotten all year.

He responded that it was for the best, but that his kids were taking it hard. I was thinking I wouldn't mind taking it hard from him anytime! A few more days, and a few more back and forth emails, followed before he finally typed, *I would love to see you again. What are you doing Saturday night?*

What was I doing Saturday night? Going out with him, of course. We did, and it was an amazing night. We talked and talked and talked into the night. We had so much in common, and there was an instant attraction. He kissed me that first night, and the rest is history.

Several months later, I was in love. *We* were in love. We spent every day that we could together. My daughter loved Alex and thought we made a "cute couple." Everything with us was great, except for two really big things: his wife and kids. The kids were not happy with the separation and were not exactly my biggest fans. The wife was constantly bashing me to him and the kids. He didn't listen, but she made an impression on her kids. She drove by my house when he was over, called him feigning a need for him, did anything and everything to get him back.

Alex and I continued to fall for each other despite these obstacles. I saw spending the rest of my life with him, and we talked about the future. . .*our* future. I told my friends, my parents, my own daughter, that this was it, that I had found the man of my dreams, and that we were going to spend the rest of our lives together. We talked about vacations, where we wanted to go and what we wanted to see together. The only thorns in our sides remained his ex-wife and, to an extent, his children, though when they were with him, they hung out with all of us and we had lots of fun. It's when they went back to their mom that the bashing started again.

Looking back, my own marriage was a mess. We should have never gotten married, and had never been happy. The only good thing that had come out of my marriage was my beautiful daughter. Alex truly could not stand his wife, and his heart had moved on, but the guilt he had over his kids was immense. They, like many, wanted their mom and dad back together and this separation had destroyed them. I tried to tell Alex that kids are resilient and will bounce back, and he wanted to believe it, hoped I was right.

Four months later, Alex told me he had a family event he had to go to. He was taking his kids, and his wife had also been invited. He had an obligation to go, he said, and wasn't happy about it, but he had to be there. We would see each other the next day.

That day, that night, something in my heart just didn't feel right. I couldn't put a finger on it, but something was off.

The next morning, I waited to hear from him, and waited, and waited. I texted him; he didn't answer. I called him, and the call went straight to voice mail. I checked Facebook—he wasn't online. Was he okay? Had he gotten hurt? Had something happened to him? I got in my car and drove to his house. Nope, not there. Starting to get nervous, I drove back home to find nothing still, no messages, no nothing.

I had work that day, and I threw myself into it, distracting myself as much as possible, but checking my Blackberry as often as I could. By the end of the night, I still had not heard from him. I went home, hopped in the shower, and settled down in front of the computer. I logged onto Facebook and checked my inbox. There were no messages from him, but I browsed his page. There were new pictures of him on it—of him, his kids. . .and his *wife?*—all at the family event that he'd said he was going to, and they all looked. . .happy. *He* looked happy. I flipped through the pictures one by one: him and the kids, him and the kids, and her, and finally. . .one of the two of them. And he looked happy. The motherfucker had posted pictures of them on Facebook, and that's how I'd found what was going on. Facebook had told me the truth.

I got in my car and drove to his house. Again, he was not there. A flashbulb popped in my head, and I drove to the house he'd once shared with them—and there, just as if the past four months had been a dream, sat his car in the driveway and all the lights off in the house. The tears come easily and strong and hard.

I don't know how, but I got myself home that night, into bed, and under my sea of covers. . .and I didn't come out for days.

Alex eventually texted and emailed and called. He didn't have to tell me, though; I knew. He's gone back, not to his wife, as he explained, but to being a family. He'd gone back for the kids.

27

FBFW

ALL I EVER WANTED in life was to do and be great—at my career, at being a father, and of course, at being a great husband. Is that too much to ask for? I strive high and always have. The goals I set out for myself to achieve have been above and beyond what one would consider realistic, and that's what's kept me going and succeeding.

I always knew I wanted a wife, a family, a sense of being. I met my wife in college, and after dating for a bit, we got married. Soon after that we had our first child. I was working a great job, my wife was by my side, and we had a beautiful child. What more could a man want in life? Life was great. . . or so I thought.

Why didn't I see it? I sometimes ask myself. Was it there and I didn't want to see it, or was it hidden so carefully that there was no way for me to see it? Eighteen years and several children later,

I learned the truth. My marriage was a sham, a lie, a match made in hell.

A few years ago, my wife started on this social networking thing, and her being on the Internet was our true downfall. Once she joined Facebook, she was already on her way to deceiving me more and more. I had my suspicions of her lies, but the last thing I wanted to do was doubt the woman I'd married and the mother of my children.

It started with her catching up with high school and college friends. Don't get me wrong. . .I do the same thing on Facebook. It's great seeing people from your past, where they are and what they turned in to, but she took it a step further.

Once she friended those she knew from her past, she started friending complete strangers. After that, there was no turning back. I don't know why she was looking for something else, but she was. She started being distant and cold to me. I knew something was going on, so I key logged her computer. I was going to catch her in the act. What I found out was the beginning to the end of our life together.

The woman who had vowed to be my wife, in sickness and in health, till death did us part, was a cheating bitch. She was sending sexual messages to people—some whom she knew from her past, and some whom she didn't know at all—and they were sending them back to her. The mother of my children was sitting there on Facebook and getting nasty with people when she would hardly get nasty with her own husband.

I confronted her with what I'd discovered. What could she say? I had proof, and she couldn't use her lies to get out of it.

Not only did she admit to these Facebook sexual interactions, but she admitted that she had been physically cheating on me.

I should have left that night. I would have if it hadn't been for my innocent, beautiful children, whose world would have come shattering down had I left. She begged me for another chance; I gave it to her. For our children, I gave her another chance—but not for me. After that night, my heart never felt the same. I would live with that heaviness for as long as I had to, to keep my family intact.

That was several years ago and, as I said, I have never felt the same since. I knew she wouldn't change. She didn't have the capacity to change, and she didn't want to. I stayed in this situation and marriage until I couldn't take it anymore.

Right after the holidays, we had it out again. When I confronted her with the suspicions that I had continued to have, she confirmed everything. She had been cheating on me this whole time, on Facebook and in real life—cheated on me right after we married, and continued to up to that very moment. She'd cheated on me before and after the births of our children, through career changes, through happiness and sadness in our lives. For fifteen out of the eighteen years we were married, she had cheated on me. With a heavy heart, I left.

All I ever wanted in life was to do and be great. I wanted to marry someone that loved me unconditionally and to be the mother of my children. My ex-wife took that away from me. I am so blessed to have my kids, but I could have been with someone who loved me for me, was honest and loyal to me, my children, our family. Instead, I wasted years and years with someone who lied every day and took me for a ride I would never want to get back on.

This person, whom I called wife, had no moral fiber. She was full of lies, full of shit. All she wanted to do was take from me and ruin my life, but guess what? In the end, she did me a favor. I am sad that I don't get to see my children every day, but I would rather be happy, honest, and complete.

My ex is an incredibly mean, bitter, and destructive person who thinks I will never find love again. Well, that's where she is wrong. I have always been a strong person, and what she did to me made me even stronger. I will love again. How dare she say I won't? As a matter of fact, there is someone special in my life, someone from my past whom I love, and guess where I found her . . .on Facebook.

The irony of it hardly escapes me. Facebook isn't what caused my marriage to fail, but it was the vehicle that led to its demise. My wife was cheating on me way before there was a Facebook, so what happened would have happened with or without it. Facebook might have been the enabler in my failed marriage, but it is also what led to my newfound life.

I will never, ever, let someone do to me what that woman did. I will trust again and love again and be in a healthy relationship again. That "C U Next Tuesday" bitch of an ex-wife will not get the best of me. I am happy and smiling again. She may be the mother of my children, but all she is to me is a FBFW—fucking bitch, fuckin' whore.

28

Hallelujah, I'm Free!

M<small>Y WIFE IS CHEATING</small> on Facebook. There! I said it out loud! And guess what? She is doing me the biggest favor ever!

Here's the deal: I'm not a harsh guy, I'm not mean. But a man has his needs, catch my drift? We've been married for an unlucky thirteen years. The passion in our marriage disappeared long ago. I've tried to make it work, tried to be encouraging to her, but no— she does not want to listen to anything I have to say.

So enter Facebook in our lives. I don't know much about it except all the kids are doing it. Our daughter wants an account so my wife helps her set one up. At the same time, she decides to set one up for herself. Twenty-four hours later, the woman is hooked and can't get off the damn thing.

Day after day, night after night, she sits in front of the computer and is on Facebook. I don't think anything of it at first, and honestly, I don't care. The more she's on Facebook, the less I have to deal with her.

One day, she runs out of the house for a quick errand and forgets to log off her Facebook account. I just happen to be walking by the computer, and it catches my eye. So, I start to read and, let me tell you, it gets interesting.

First of all, she uses a picture of herself from right when we met. We're talking fifty pounds lighter and fifteen years younger. What is that fat whore thinking, I ask myself, using an old picture of herself? What's she gonna do if she ever meets up with these people in person? Hire a model to play her?

I then notice that she has been talking to the guy she dated in high school—her "schweet heart," she used to call him. I think I just threw up in my mouth. If she is talking to Mr. Schmuck— what *I* call him—something fishy must be going on.

Now, look, for years this woman has accused me of having affairs though I have been as faithful as a nun to her church. I have provided absolutely everything for that woman, and now I'm reading flirtatious messages between her and her ex.

> *You know what I remember most about you baby,*
> *it's the way you liked to be tickled right between those*
> *legs of yours,* he's typed.
> *You have an excellent memory. I remember how*
> *good you were at tickling,* she answers.
> *I miss your rockin' body.*

She hasn't responded to him yet, and I don't know how the

hell she is *going* to respond, since all the rocking her body does is rock the house with its weight!

So what do I do? I wait for her to come home and confront her. Yes, siree, ma'am, I am not gonna let her do this under my nose, near my kids, in my house. No way, no how! When she comes home, I'm sitting right in front of her computer. At first, she accuses, me, *me*, of hacking into her account and snooping on her. Umm, excuse me, I'm no hacker, but leaving an open computer still logged on makes it real easy to snoop. I won't deny that.

She sheds the requisite tears and tells me she's sorry, but she's confused. Well, I'm not confused at all. Either you want to be in this marriage, or you don't. Either you want me, Ray, your husband, the one who you swore on a bible till death do us part, or you don't. There should be no confusion. It should be plain and simple, I tell her.

I've been by her side, I have stuck it out, through her unhappiness, her weight gain, her bitterness. I stayed true, but I can't say the same for her. And guess what? She is doing me the biggest favor ever. Mr. Schmuck is doing me the biggest favor ever. Confused, she says? There should be no confusion, and the answer is right in front of me. What a gift. What a blessing—finally an excuse for me to leave her. There is a light at the end of the tunnel and I can finally be happy.

So, yes, my wife is cheating on Facebook. But all I can say is, Hallelujah, I'm free! Thank you, Facebook.

29

The Power of Facebook

I HAD A FACEBOOK AFFAIR. Actually, to call it an affair so minimizes what it really was. True, it was an affair, but it was a love affair, an affair that you would think would surpass any obstacles—so strong, so powerful, that one's heart would lead the way and help make decisions and changes in one's life.

I was married. He was married. It lasted a summer and ended as quickly as it had begun.

We knew each other from our younger years and reconnected on Facebook. What started as a night of chatting turned into a face-to-face meeting and a torrid and intense affair. Falling in love with this new person made me realize how very badly I wanted to end my marriage and start something new.

It was a summer of love, lust, making love, fucking hard. It was a summer of *rendez-vouses*, hotel trysts, messy beds, sheets all over, condom wrappers on the floor, putting the cell phone on vibrate, ignoring the outside world, and conversations about the future.

We knew, both of us knew, the affair was more than just that. It was a love that neither of us could describe or explain, that was all about timing and taking it one day at a time—a love that we knew, we would always have but might not necessarily be able to act upon at the current time. We knew we had found each other once again, and that one day we would grow old together.

It started on Facebook. It ended on its own, yet, it the end, the very end, it was Facebook once again that made the impact.

I had over ten years under my belt and a few kids. He too had been married for a while but had no kids. I would ask him, "Are you happy? Truly happy?" He couldn't answer that. His wife wanted a kid. He wasn't so sure. Yet he was planning to give her what she wanted.

In between the incredible sex and love, our conversations were intense. We talked about today. We talked about tomorrow. We talked about yesterday. He promised that he would never let me go. We had lost touch for so many years and, no matter what, he promised, I would always be a part of his life.

I remember one night, the last we ever had together, sitting with him, talking to him, holding him, looking at him. I had said it before and I said it again: "When you have kids, when *she* gets pregnant, everything will change." He assured me it wouldn't. But I am a mom. I know. I assured him it would. "When *she* gets pregnant, I will lose you." He promised me he would never lose me again.

That last night together was the most intense; it made us realize how so much more of a relationship ours had become, and it changed everything.

Whether he realized it or not, after that, he pushed me away. He was busy with work, and although we still spoke, he did not make the time to meet. I started dating, doing my thing, but always knew, and always told him, he was my soul mate. We were meant to be together, I said, and he never ever disagreed.

When we didn't talk, my only way of knowing what was going on in his life was through Facebook. Every day, multiple times a day, I would check his page. Who had he friended? Who was writing on his wall? What pictures was he posting and being tagged in? Yes, I became a Facebook stalker, lurker, whatever you want to call it.

He was the kind of Facebook guy who controlled what was on his wall. If someone posted a picture on it and he didn't like it, he took it off. Those silly applications that people send— you know, blessings, a martini, flowers—he deleted those right away too. When that kind of stuff stayed on his wall, I knew how busy he was at work.

We still talked from time to time, usually by text or email. I knew he was trying to be a "good boy," and he kept telling me we needed to meet, to be face to face, for him to explain how he felt about everything. I continued to ask him if his wife was pregnant. *Not to my knowledge,* he told me. I told *him* to go have his family, have his kid or two, and he would see that having kids doesn't fix a marriage. It doesn't make things happy. Once you have kids, there is no turning back. As amazing and wonderful as they are, kids change things. Marriages, relationships, never stay the same.

Deep down inside, I knew it would happen. It was inevitable. When two people keep actively fucking with no protection, usually a pregnancy will occur. It was what he wanted for *her*.

I just never thought I would find out the way I did.

As I said, we still had communication. It wasn't the way it had been, but I got the texts about him missing me, dreaming of me, remembering us.

Then even this communication nearly stopped. Every now and then I would get a little "hi" on my phone, but for the most part, all contact ended. I wrote it off by telling myself he was busy, the holidays were coming, he must be traveling. Looking back now, I realize I must have known.

One afternoon, I was on the Facebook home page; as it refreshes, the live feed comes on. I saw that he'd been tagged in some pictures. A friend of his had tagged them. I also saw the pictures were recent. I clicked on them and saw him and his wife. One look at her, and I knew. Call it women's intuition. It was her look, her outfit, his expression next to her. She was pregnant. Of course, I had no proof, and I scanned his wall for any notices of congratulations I might have missed. I found nothing.

I logged off Facebook and helped my kids with their homework. My temper with them was on a short fuse. This disturbed me, and I went back to look at the pictures again. I didn't know who posted them, but I was soon able to view the entire album where the pictures came from. There are a lot of them—none of my guy, but I kept looking, until I stopped: There she was. His wife. This time I knew for sure—I knew the look. I know it before I even read the caption under the picture.

My heart dropped. My stomach churned. A feeling of nausea passed over me. The tears flowed and wouldn't stop, even though I had known that day would come. I wasn't surprised, but shocked.

So what had started on Facebook ended on Facebook. To have had what we had, heard the things he said to me, do the things we had, and to find out she was pregnant on Facebook: Nothing could come closer than a slap in the face.

That he didn't have the decency, the courage, to tell me himself, really hurt. That was why I had not heard from him. I'd predicted it, warned him it would happen though he promised me it wouldn't. I had found out on Facebook that the man I loved, the man I hoped to be my future, was going to be a dad.

I was heartbroken—not because she'd become pregnant, but because he hadn't told me himself. I was owed that.

He was, in fact, a coward, a pussy, a sell-out. Yes, I have cried many tears. Yes, I am in shock. And yes, I must move on, enable this to make me stronger and move forward. It's all I can do.

I sent him a private message on Facebook letting him know I *knew*, congratulating him on the news, wishing his wife the best. I took the high road and, as much as it hurts, I'm proud that I did.

30

Damn You

DAMN YOU FOR BEING on Facebook that night.

Damn you for answering me.

Damn you for telling me you always had a thing for me.

Damn you for forgetting your wife that night.

Damn you for being married.

Damn you for wanting to see me.

Damn you for all those late night chats.

Damn you for making me fall in love with you the moment we saw each other again.

Damn you for making me feel the way I feel.

Damn you for making me feel special.

Damn you for making me think we had a chance.

Damn you for allowing me to believe in you.

Damn you for allowing me to believe in us.

Damn you for making me think we had a future.

Damn you for making me sit by the phone and wait.

Damn you for making me sit by Facebook and wait.

Damn you for making me shed tears when I think of you.

Damn you for making me still wonder what could have been.

Damn you for not taking that leap of faith.

Damn you for making promises you never kept.

Damn you for holding me, kissing me, and loving me.

Damn you for making me come the way I did.

Damn you for telling me I took you to a place that is magical.

Damn you for making me think you were my knight in shining armor.

Damn you for loving me.

Damn you for letting me love you.

Damn!

Damn you, damn you, damn you.

Part Five

Falling in Like n' Love—
Facebook Style

IN SOME CASES, FACEBOOK can become something more lastingly positive than frivolous fun. Some people find experiences and parts of themselves they never would have uncovered without this unique website. These romances, when they work out—even temporarily—pack real-life punch. Dating your high school girlfriend makes you feel younger than driving a Porsche. It's intoxicating. Like any affairs, these can grow into a real relationship or fizzle like a typical romance. The ones that grow into something real are as real as any relationship.

What follows are some of these like n' love stories. This section is about the handful of Facebook affairs that have potential to grow into something real and ultimately end happily (or not). After all, is there really such thing as a happily ever after?

31

MTK 403

LEIGH: YOU'RE SUCH A *Facebook whore!*

Jason: *What's that supposed to mean?*

Leigh: *You know exactly what it means. You're a Facebook whore. You're one of those people who are always on, always updating your status, always commenting on other people's statuses.*

Jason: *And what does that make you?*

Leigh: *Do you see me complaining? That's what brought us together again. It was 'cause of my status that we are where we are today. You know that, right?*

Jason: *I know. You wrote a status, I commented, you commented back and the rest is history.*

Leigh: *I've kept all of our Facebook emails. I have them from day one. . .the very first day we had that conver-*

sation. I wish I had all our chats, too.

Jason: *Oh, baby, the chats are all here. In our hearts.*

Leigh: *See, this is why I love this guy. Such a romantic. It's because of Facebook that I found love again. Didn't expect it at all—at least not that fast and certainly not with him.*

Jason: *Thanks a lot.*

Leigh: *You know what I mean. We went to high school together. Grew up together. But we went our separate ways after we graduated. I had heard things about you through the years. Did you keep tabs on me?*

Jason: *Ha-ha. Once a while your name came up, but I was busy doing my thing.*

Leigh: *We were both busy doing our things. Getting married, having kids. . .we didn't see each other for like twenty years.*

Jason: *Until our twenty-year high school reunion.*

Leigh: *We only talked for a minute.*

Jason: *Honey, we were all so busy that night. Catching up with everyone.*

Leigh: *Trust me. I was pretty busy myself.*

Jason: *But we took a picture together. See, babe, I was into you even then.*

Leigh: *It was a group picture and we happen to be at the same table. Plus, you were married, I was married, and hooking up with each other was the last thing on our minds that night. In fact, if I were to hook up, I had my eye on—*

Jason: *We don't need to get into that, do we?*

Leigh: *Are you jealous? You are so cute. My heart is only for you Jay. So anyways, yes, we reconnected at the reunion.*

Jason: *And at that point, everyone was getting on Facebook so, of course, we became Facebook friends.*

Leigh: *I don't think we ever had Facebook conversations. Maybe you would like my status every now and then, but that's about it. I think you once liked my status I wrote that I was glad Howard Stern was back from vacation.*

Jason: *I'm sure I did. And I know we wished each other happy birthday.*

Leigh: *Well, everyone does that. But I do remember seeing a lot of your status updates. I also remember seeing your relationship status change.*

Jason: *You did? I don't know if you've ever told me that.*

Leigh: *Yeah. I remember seeing it change and knowing you were getting divorced. But I didn't know you well enough to email you about it—seemed too personal to comment on.*

Jason: *But I emailed you when I saw your status.*

Leigh: *Yeah, but that was different. It wasn't a relationship status change. I wrote something, you commented, I commented back, and then you popped me up in chat.*

Jason: *Well, I could tell something was going on with you.*

Something was off. Not right.

Leigh: *Well, you were right. My husband and I had just separated. We'd ended up having a long conversation that day. You'd told me what you were going through, and also that, if I ever needed a friend, you'd be there for me.*

Jason: *It was my way of flirting with you.*

Leigh: *Like I said, you were being a friend. And I appreciated it. And yes, you were flirting. It felt good. I knew then that maybe I still had something. Maybe I wasn't this washed-up, almost-forty, minivan-driving mama.*

Jason: *First of all, you are beautiful. Yes, you drive the minivan and are an amazing mama, but washed up? Not the word I would use to describe you.*

Leigh: *Awww, you are the sweetest. So, we became fast Facebook friends. We flirted a lot, we chatted a lot, we emailed a lot, we commented on each other's statuses a lot.*

Jason: *Our relationship—well, friendship—began and continued all on Facebook.*

Leigh: *I love when you comment on my status and it's just us. . .back and forth. . .commenting together.*

Jason: *Why do we do that? I just thought of that. . .why do we even do that?*

Leigh: *Because that's who we are. Facebook is what started this, and we both are into it. It's who we are. We don't say anything too private, too embarrassing, too revealing. And a lot of it is just us. . .in our language.*

Jason: *Like MTK 403.*

Leigh: *Like MTK 403.*

Jason: *You have this ex-boyfriend. This guy you dated in college who we both know. We all went to high school together. And he has a thing for you.*

Leigh: *You don't know that.*

Jason: *Please. The guy is always commenting all over your wall. So, one night we're chatting, and I see this guy comment on your status. And then he signs his comment with an "x" and "o." A kiss and hug. . . "xo." Now, for a month, I've been signing all of my notes to you, private notes, with an "x" an "o."*

Leigh: *And you refused to share an "x" and "o" with this guy.*

Jason: *It just minimized it to me. It didn't seem as special now that he was using it, too. So, I said we need to come up with our own letters for a hug and a kiss.*

Leigh: *You just put in random letters and it was "MK."*

Jason: *That's right. "MK." It's two letters that were close to the return button on the keyboard. They just so happened to be "M" and "K." So that's what we used for a few days.*

Leigh: *Instead of the "x" and "o" it was "M" and "K." And then we said, Well, what if want more than just a hug and kiss? What if we want to add tongue to it?*

Jason: *So we put the "T" in there. . . . It's a kiss and hug with tongue in the middle.*

Leigh: *And the 403. . . .*

Jason: *That was the hotel room number where we first did the nasty.*

Leigh: *Very funny. We really are cute, aren't we?*

Jason: *It's probably one of the more G-rated things we have done on Facebook. All I can say is Facebook sex is better than you would think.*

Leigh: *Jason!*

Jason: *It's true. I mean, having real sex is the best. But if you can't have it, and the only other thing available is a laptop and your hand, well, the rest is history. There's nothing like typing to your girl to put their hand down their pants and rub themselves—*

Leigh: *I think they get the point. You know what I love about Facebook. . .it's that you are always logged on. Even though you're at work and you just have it on your screen, you're still there. Just seeing your name online, well, everyday, it makes me feel closer to you. Like I know you are on the other side of that computer screen.*

Jason: *Now it's your turn to be the romantic. And when you see me on the other side of that chat screen, nine times out of ten, you are playing with yourself, right? Give me at least that visual to think about.*

Leigh: *Anything for you, baby. On Facebook, anything for you.*

32

Jack and Jill Went Up the Hill and Got Laid

JILL: IT WAS CUTE *when we were younger. . .Jack and Jill went up the hill. . .everyone would say it to us.*

Jack: *All of our friends teased us when we dated.*

Jill: *We were only, what, fourteen, fifteen years old, but it seemed like so much more. We did everything together and had so much fun. Those high school years were the best.*

Jack: *They were great.*

Jill: *But, of course, all good things come to an end. Something happened, some high school drama, and then it was over between us. I don't even remember what it was. Do you, honey?*

Jack: *No, I don't. It was probably some he said, she said, kind of shit.*

Jill: *I'm sure. High school drama, just like I said. That's how important it was. . .we don't even remember what our breakup was about! Anyways, we both ended up dating other people and went our separate ways.*

Jack: *And lost touch.*

Jill: *And lost touch.*

Jill: *We both ended up marrying our college sweethearts and settling down. I have two kids, and you have three.*

Jack: *Can you believe we lived in the same city, close to where we grew up, and never ever ran into each other.*

Jill: *Never, ever. . .until—*

Jack: *Until. It was getting close to our thirtieth high school reunion, and everyone was getting on Facebook to get back in touch and find everyone.*

Jill: *I still remember the day I found you on Facebook. I had just joined and was starting to friend people, and then I saw you. We both were friends with Charlie. I think my heart skipped a beat when I asked you to be my friend, and it skipped even more beats when you accepted.*

Jack: *I remember when I saw you on Facebook. Baby, I was never the same again!*

Jill: *You're embarrassing me.*

Jack: *What's to be embarrassed? You're a beautiful woman, and I don't know why we ever broke it off in the first place! What an ass I was!*

Jill: *We started talking on Facebook. At first, it was polite and platonic—about high school, our friends, who we keep in touch with, our kids, our lives.*

Jack: *And then something turned one night. We took it a step further.*

Jill: *That we did. Look, I loved my husband, but I had not been happy for a long time. I felt, when I talked to you, that I was the happiest I had ever been. You made me remember who I was and what it was like to be me.*

Jack: *My marriage was falling apart, and chatting with you on Facebook made me have a smile on my face again.*

Jill: *But we decided to wait for the reunion to see each other. We both went, without our spouses, of course, and—*

Jack: *And the moment you walked into the room I felt fifteen again. I knew, right when I saw you, I could never let you go again.*

Jill: *We ended up spending that whole night together. Talking into the night. And we knew from that moment on, our lives would never be the same again.*

Jack: *That was a year ago.*

Jill: *And what a year it's been.*

33

The Grandfather Clause

THEN: NOVEMBER, 1991.

I was twenty, he was twenty-one. We were family friends, sorta. Our parents had grown up together, but we didn't hang out much in our growing years. Obviously, we knew who we were and would run into each other from time to time, but that's about it—until a family brunch one day in November. I saw him. He saw me. We must have exchanged numbers, because that night I got the booty call—I mean phone call—and I didn't hesitate to go over. And that night we fucked again and again.

I didn't know him well, but, man, oh man, was he a hottie. I was a senior in college looking for love in all the wrong places and had nothing to lose.

The next night, I get the same call, and I did the same thing. There was an attraction, but he was clear that this is basically where it would start and end. He didn't want a girlfriend, he just wanted to fuck, and that we did.

About two months later, I ended up meeting the man who would eventually become my husband, so that fuck fest was just another one for the books, one more to add to my list.

The funny thing is, in all my single years, the one thing I was always very proud of was that I'd never had a one-night stand. This fuck, though, was my closest thing to it—a guy who, despite the fact we had "family history," I hardly knew. For me, that's a one-night stand (or two, I should say).

Through the years, whenever I did a fuck-roll call or his name came up in conversation, I would think about him and our two nights. I also would think, you know, if he walked past me down the street, I didn't know if I would even recognize him. So, yes, for me, he was my one night, two-night stand. And yes, it was hot.

Now: Summer, 2010

My life has been a rollercoaster, to say the least. A Mom to two kids, I was in an unhappy marriage. I decided to take the jump and separated from my husband. I'm not sure where this is all going to go, but I'm following my heart, my gut, my instinct, seeing where it takes me.

I was out with my girlfriends one night—wow, almost a year ago—when one mentioned that a mutual friend was now on Facebook. He was also getting divorced and already seeing someone else. That mutual friend was my one-night, two-night stand.

So I friended him. . .of course I did. And guess what—he denied! Shot me down. WTF? I'd fucked the guy almost twenty years before, but he wouldn't be my Facebook friend?

Time went by, maybe nine months. One day I logged onto Facebook, and, lo and behold, there was a friend request—from him. Whoa! Change of heart? I'm not one to hold a grudge, so I accepted. I also sent him a note, one or two lines, asking how the hell he was. I got no response. This guy, I told myself, is something else.

One night, on Facebook as usual, I saw him online. Third time is the charm, right? So I popped him up, and within ten seconds he responded, and our friendship began. It happened pretty fast, but for us, I guess that was par for the course.

Within minutes of the *how are you* and *how's the family*, we got down to business. He brought up our one- night, two-night. I confirmed it. We figured out that his cock had been the last one in me before I met my husband. What a bond we had.

And then he did it—pulled out from under his cape, drum roll please, the Grandfather Clause.

> *You know we have the Grandfather Clause on our side. We should get together,* he says.
>
> *Grandfather Clause?* I ask.
>
> *I'm Grandfathered in. Being with me doesn't count, since we've been there done that. It doesn't change your count, and we already know it's gonna be hot,* he reasoned.
>
> *Hmmmm....very, very interesting argument,* I replied.

I slept on it. Maybe the guy had a point. We'd already fucked. We knew it was gonna be good. He's right, I thought—it doesn't mess with my count, since he won't be a newbie. Maybe, just maybe that's the reason for our one-night, two-night so long ago.

The next morning I sent him a Facebook message, reading simply:

> *two thumbs up for the grandfather clause. . .the more i think about it, the more i likey. . .i say we go for it. . .*

So we did.

I got a sitter for the kids and went to his house two days later. He opened the door, and, within minutes, we knew there was some kind of something going on.

He wanted to take a swim; I joined him outside. I stayed at the edge, feet dangling in. We talked, we drank a little, we smoked a little. I was flirting a lot (I am known to be good at that). I told him I knew he wanted to kiss me. He said he did.

I beckoned him to my lips, and we kissed and kissed and kissed—awesome, sensual, fireworks in the sky, tingly in all the right places.

After a while, we went up to his room. A little buzzed from the weed, the wine, and the chemistry we couldn't deny, we settled into bed and started again, just where we'd left off. And it was better than ever. Pretty fucking hot, I have to say, this grandfather sex.

During one of our breaks, I checked my phone, and we

laughed as I changed my Facebook status to:

Big fan of the grandfather clause.

I have a feeling this grandfather thing is gonna be more than a one-night, two-night. Who knows where it's going to go, but I'm having a hell of a time with the grandfather.

34

18 Again

YOU READ ABOUT IT. You hear about it. You daydream about it. You know it can happen and it has happened. You just so want it to happen to you. I know I'm one of the lucky ones, because that thing you want so badly happened to me.

You know how the saying goes. . .it usually happens when you least expect it, when you truly don't think it's going to. It's sorta like love at first sight, but you don't quite want to rush to judgment and think it's love. It's more like a *like*, a *like* that is different from your average *like,* one that is powerful, full of chemistry, fireworks, like that magnetic force on *Lost*. In fact, I *am* lost—lost in *like.*

There I was, minding my own business, talking to my friend, doing my thing, and he walked up, said hello, sat down, and the rest is history.

We knew each other, though not well. We had gone to the same high school, had some friends in common, but were years apart. I'd always known who he was, though actually, to be perfectly honest, he hardly remembered me. Thanks a lot.

At the suggestion of my good friend, I had sent him a Facebook friend request just weeks earlier. He was single. I was newly single.

We talked as if we had been great friends for years. We had the same thoughts, the same humor. He got me. I got him. He made me smile.

We tried to guess how many Facebook friends we had in common. I said twenty-four. He said twenty-seven. We had twenty-eight.

The whole interaction lasted, what, two hours? People were coming and going around us, and there we still were, sitting and talking.

I was going out with a friend later that night, and I asked him to join us. He had plans, with a girl, though, someone he just had started dating a few weeks earlier. Still, he asked for my number. I told him to just find me on Facebook. "Uh, no," he said. "I'm calling you." Within three hours of our meeting, the texting began. It went on through the night. It was sporadic, though, and I knew why. He was with the girl. I joked to him he was texting me at her bathroom breaks. He LOL'd. . .I was right.

I went on Facebook the next day and checked out his profile, got to know him from his posts and pictures. I liked what I saw.

He went out of town on business that week, and our friendship turned into something more—from our texts and phone calls, we realized, a lot more than we had bargained for, a lot more than two friends getting reacquainted. We had something that people hope for, that only comes around once in a while, and that we knew we couldn't ignore. We felt like teenagers, eighteen again.

But there was one problem: The other girl was still around.

He knew what he had to do, though, that it was us, not them.

We counted down the days until he came home and had a first date that would last for hours—a quick bite to eat and a walk to the beach, and all we did was talk and kiss and kiss and talk. Yes, we knew we had something.

Flash forward, one week, two weeks, three weeks. We both knew how very good it was, yet that "but" remained. He had not ended it with *her* yet.

I pushed him away once, told him I couldn't share him. That didn't last long. I came back, ready and willing to fight for what I believed in.

He went on another trip, and another, and the whole time he was telling me it was me. . .it was us. Yet she was still around. Why? I don't know. But he couldn't let her go, or me.

It finally ended. It had to. As much as my heart believed in us, I couldn't do it anymore. I wanted him with me. He never really gave us a fair chance. And so we were done.

The whole summer was a sad one. He was the one I wanted to be with. Something kept tugging my heart. He and I were *not* done. We had unfinished business.

We live in a small town, and I heard he'd met her parents. To me, that sealed the deal. Once they meet the parents, well, it signifies a lot. I dated others, but I could only compare. No one made me feel the way he had.

That connection we had doesn't come along every day. I just hoped I would find it again—someone who got me, someone I got, who was me and whom I was.

We ran into each other a few times that summer. We exchanged quick hellos. I couldn't stop for more. The only connection we had was Facebook. I would check his page daily for any hint into his life. I also would check her page. . . waiting for a relationship status change to happen.

By the time the summer was ending, I had met someone else—again, someone from my past. I liked him, but he was not the person I truly wanted to be with. He also wasn't in the place to commit to anyone. Though we started spending time together and there was something between us, it wasn't even close to what I'd felt with the one who made me smile.

And then the unexpected happened, the thing you hope for, have been praying for every night.

Bing. My text sound went off, and it was him.

It was a Wednesday night. He wanted to tell me the news. *The news?*

Of course, I thought the worst—they'd gotten engaged. And if that was the case, all my hurt was worth it. Because in the end, all I wanted, was for him to be happy. That's the truth, because that's how much I cared.

But the news was just the opposite. They had broken up.

> *Why?* I asked.
> *I wasn't happy. She wasn't you,* he replied.

Since then we have taken it slow. We have seen each other a lot. No labels. No status changes. Slow and low, that is the tempo.

It's still all there, though—our connection, our chemistry. No one makes me feel the way he does. We are eighteen again.

35

Long-Distance Love Affair

IT STARTED OFF INNOCENTLY enough: one friend reaching out to another. We were both going through the same thing at the same time. Both of our marriages were ending, and we were friends from elementary school reaching out to help each other: a status comment here, a Facebook chat there. We never thought it would go farther than that, especially since we were living on opposite coasts. But of course, things happen when you least expect them to.

He came to town, and we knew at first glance that this was much more than a Facebook friendship, flirt, or fuck. We spent days together developing something in person. We wrote goofy status updates that only we would understand. We acted as a couple, visiting with high school friends and spending every moment that we could together.

Then he went back home.

I couldn't stand not seeing him, so I flew to see him for another weekend filled with great meals, great conversation, and insane sexual chemistry.

The next few months were hard. We had no plans to see each other, no physical contact, just Facebook, Skype, texting, and the phone.

We decided to spend the holidays together. We spent another great few days together. By then, we knew how much more our relationship had grown. It was love, something that could last forever. . .except for one thing. How could forever happen when we had an entire continent between us?

As a result, we made a decision we didn't want to make. It had to end, not because we wanted it to but because it had to. It hurt too much to keep going day after day and know we couldn't come home to each other physically.

What happens on Facebook now? We love each other and will remain friends, but can we be Facebook friends? Can we tolerate watching our private lives unfold on Facebook, knowing we are not part of them? When a girl flirts with him on his wall or a guy sends me an "xo" on mine, how do we handle that? We don't want to block each other, because we are still great friends and want to be part of each other's lives.

I just went onto his page, and already a girl, whom I don't know, has sent him good wishes. I can't say a thing, can't act jealous, but it hurts. I want him back. I want us to work this thing out.

Maybe there will be a someday. Maybe one day we can restart it again. What started as Facebook friends is ending the same way. We have come full circle.

36

Sparkles and Glimmers

ALWAYS HAD A THING for her. There was a sparkle in her eye, a glimmer in her smile, and a warmth that radiated from her whole being. We went steady for a blip of a second in middle school, one of many girls I actually dated, but this one made an impact, left something on my heart.

We continued to be friends in high school. I dated her best friend, and she had a serious boyfriend. We would double date, the four of us, and we spent days, nights, weekends together—always friends, always friendly, but in the back of my heart and mind I knew there was more.

After high school, we went our separate ways. I would think about her through the years, wondering where she was, who she ended up with, but we never crossed paths—until Facebook.

I'd only joined Facebook as a recommendation from a colleague at work. I really didn't expect a thing out of it. In fact, I hardly checked or went on it. I didn't upload a profile picture, and I only had a few friends, all work related—until *she* found me.

The message was simple.

Is this you? she asked.

I wrote back that it was me and how glad I was that she had found me.

We were both married to others and had children of our own. We lived in the same state, but not close by. Although twenty years had passed since we last saw each other, I felt that tug in my heart as soon as I saw that first email in my inbox.

We spent that summer emailing back and forth. I put up a profile picture and posted pictures of my life. I looked at her pictures and saw that sparkle, that glimmer in her smile that was still there. She brought me back into the world of high school, and I quickly became friends with many of our friends from the past.

The timing was impeccable, since our reunion was soon approaching. We ended up sitting next to each other and spent the whole night talking. It was as friends, of course, but I can't deny it: There was an attraction, after all those years, still.

After the reunion we didn't speak much—a few back-and-forth messages on Facebook, but that's about it, until one summer night that changed my life forever.

It was late; I had just had a long day of work. I was truly ready to turn in for the night. My wife and kids were already asleep, and I just wanted to go on Facebook for a quick minute to check my emails.

She popped me up right away.

Hey! Saw you online. . .how are you? she wrote.

I read her message a few times over. I was really tired and wasn't sure if I was in the mood to have a conversation, but it was *her*. *She* was emailing me: the girl with the sparkle and glimmer.

Hey! Great to hear from you! I typed.

My heart had won out over my tired body. The conversation started very friendly, very safe. And then it happened. I don't know what it was, probably the memory of the sparkle and glimmer, but I typed something that changed me, us, forever.

That night, at the reunion. You looked great.
You know I felt something there, between us, I
typed.

There was a pause in the conversation. What the hell did I do? I asked myself. Why did I type that? I love my wife. I believe in monogamy. I believe in being faithful. I believe in being true. I've believe all those things, until now.

I felt it too, she typed.

Minutes turned into hours, and by the end of the conversation, we decided to meet in a few days.

That whole week we texted and emailed but never spoke. We flirted, we shared, we dreamed. I wanted our first words to be in person. I wanted to hear her voice when I was looking in her eyes. Was this just a Facebook fling—or more?

The day came. The moment I saw her, I knew I still had her in my heart and soul. Our eyes met, and we were lost.

That summer was *our* summer of romance, rendezvouses, and getting together any chance we could get. We went to dinners, ordered room service, lay in bed, laughed, talked, drank, kissed, and made love over and over again. Never have I had a woman make me feel the way she did. Not my wife, not anyone.

That summer, she ended up leaving her husband. Did she do it for me? Part of me thinks she did. I never made those kind of promises to *her*, though. I thought about it and, trust me, a part of me wanted to spend every day for the rest of my life with this woman. Yet I have guilt. I love my wife. I don't know if I'm *in love* with her, but I love her. She is my friend, and I'm afraid to hurt my friend.

My romance with this woman was incredible. Each time was better than the last. I wanted to be with her as much as I could, and I had to figure it out—between my work, my wife, my life.

It was Labor Day, and I was working like a dog. I missed her; it had been several weeks since our last meeting. I texted her and asked if we could meet. She arranged a hotel close to me.

I was feeling under the weather when I got to the hotel—so strange, since I had been feeling great all day and then, *bang!* I get ready to meet her and I feel like shit. I didn't know if this was going to be another one of our great nights, because I felt like crap. Maybe it was a sign that I shouldn't be doing such things.

She led me to the couch, put me in her arms and took care of me. She ordered me alphabet soup from the kid's room service menu to make me feel better. She caressed my hair, my head, my face.

After my soup, I felt a little better, and things started to get hot and heavy. We always, always, used condoms when we made love. Once, when we were in the shower, we started to make love and I stopped it right away. I just didn't feel right about it. But that night, I don't know, something was different. I wanted to feel her like I had never felt her.

I entered her, and the moment I did, it became so clear—we both gasped with pleasure and realized the incredible magnetic connection we had. Wow. I'd slept with numerous women, my wife included and never, ever, felt what I felt at that moment. We were one. I know it sounds corny, but man, we were one. I now completely get it when people say that.

We made love until she came and then she took me in her mouth until I did. That night changed it all. That summer we had had amazing times, but this raised the bar. It was how I wanted to be, wanted to live, forever.

I was going away on business the next week, and I proposed that we meet in Paris. I wanted to be with her and couldn't think of a better place than the most romantic city in the world, where no one knew us, and we could walk the streets hand in hand and create our own memories. I begged her to seriously consider it. I could make it happen and wanted her to do the same. She said yes. And my mind started planning away.

The next morning we parted ways and texted each other the whole drive home, discussing Paris and our incredible night together.

I don't know what happened after that—or, to be more precise, do but don't. I went back to work, home, reality. She was on my mind constantly, every day. Nothing had changed except that that night had made it more real and that scared me. She texted and emailed me through the week, asking about Paris. And I flaked.

I went away on my business trip and never made the plan. I just left her hanging until the day we were supposed to go to Paris. I texted her. I was an asshole. I screwed up. I hurt her. I should have gone. I should have taken her and I didn't. I was scared. I'm trying to go back to my old life. LBH—life before *her*. But it is so hard. I know I owe her more and I just can't give her more.

Here I am, trying to be the dutiful husband and father, and my heart just isn't there. I want both worlds. I want to be the good guy. I don't want to be a guy who leaves his wife. I feel terrible about it. Yet I am happiest when I think about her, when I'm with her, happiest when we are together, and I just hope one day we can be together and it's not too late.

Since that night, the night that changed it all, I have not seen her, though we have emailed and Facebooked. I love her, but I have not told her. I want to be with her, but I have not said so. I'm too scared.

We text about how much we care, how much we miss, how

much we know we are meant to be together.

It's my own fault. I can only blame myself. It's not fair to her or to my wife or to me. I need to figure this thing out before it's too late and more people get hurt. I need to grow some balls, not be afraid, and follow my heart—so much easier said than done.

37

Simply Amazing

I joined Facebook, ironically, with the encouragement of my husband. Little did I know my life was about to change.

From day one, I started searching for people from my past. I had always wanted to have a connection with people from my past and was curious to know where they were and what they were doing. My twenty-year high school reunion was also coming up. It was the perfect time to start finding people.

I remember sitting down at my computer and typing in names to see if anyone popped up. I looked for my childhood best friends, friends from camp, college friends, and, of course, friends from elementary and high school. One of the names I typed in was that of a guy I grew up with. Let's call him Ross.

I'd known him since high school. We'd hung out in the same circle and always were close. After we graduated, we had lost touch, and, every now then, he would pop into my mind. I did the Facebook move and "friended" him. Was this the same Ross I knew? Would he accept my friend request? Would he remember me? I didn't have to wait long to find out.

A few days later he emailed me. It *was* the right Ross, and he was thrilled to hear from me. We caught up with our personal lives (he was newly married; I was married with kids) and the gossip about what all our high school friends were doing. When I told him about our reunion, he was very excited to get the details. We exchanged emails and numbers and promised each other we would keep in touch and meet for the reunion.

The reunion was a weekend of fun. The night before, a bunch of us had an impromptu party. Ross called to tell me he was in town and said we should go to the party together. He was going solo, but his wife was coming in the next night.

What I remember most is seeing him, sitting down together, and talking a lot. I don't know what it was, but I definitely felt something, an attraction. I am married, but I know as we sat and talked, our legs touched a few times, as did our arms. So there was some sort of electricity, but I wasn't in a place to identify or label it.

After that, Ross stayed on my mind. Months passed; every now and then, I would see his face pop up on Facebook. A picture would post, someone would make a comment, and he continued to linger in my mind.

On Father's Day, I had another bout of late-night Facebooking. Close to midnight—I always keep my chat window open—I suddenly saw Ross online. I don't know why, but something happened inside me. I contemplated sending him a message for a quick ten seconds before I decided, What the hell, and said hi. I remember making it very casual, very innocent, and saying something about "hope you guys are well"—purposely saying "you guys" so as to include his wife. It took a minute or so, but he responded.

Our conversation was very typical—two friends saying hi, what's been going on, etc. Then something happened. I don't know how or why or what, but there was a moment when the conversation turned. Something shifted, and everything changed: Ross and I both realized that this was more than your run-of-the-mill friendly conversation. I wasn't sure what that meant yet, but, once the groundwork was set, there was no turning back. We both realized and said things that we knew were true, and we couldn't deny our feelings. That night, we chatted for hours on Facebook.

In just a short amount of time, and with hundreds and thousands of words typed between us, we knew one thing—we had to see each other in person. It was a Sunday; we decided to do so that coming Friday.

We shared intimate thoughts, laughs, and dreams the whole week on Facebook. We had no idea what was going to happen, but we had to see.

Through Facebook we got to know each other. We looked at each other's pictures, memorized each other's faces, and stared into each other's eyes. We had lots of friends in common, and I wonder how all of them would have reacted if they'd known about our Facebook "friendship".

The week crawled by at a snail's pace, but finally the day arrived and we would see each other face to face. We decided to meet at a big-name hotel near our local airport that we knew would be filled with travelling businessmen and tourists. Not a chance we would run into anyone we knew.

Our cars pulled up just about the same time; we entered the hotel and stopped in the lobby. The moment we turned and looked at each other, the moment our eyes met, I knew, *we* knew, it was more than a Facebook flirt. In fact, when we look back and talk about this first moment, it is at that moment, that he knew and I knew this was It.

We weren't sure what our next move would be—get a drink in the hotel bar, or a room for a few hours? We decided on the latter.

We rode up in the elevator giggling like two teenagers the whole way. We couldn't stop looking at each other and smiling. The room was a typical airport hotel room, but to us it could have been a suite, because all we cared about was being alone and together.

We will never forget the moment we shared our first kiss. I know it's cliché, but those fireworks went off for both of us. We kissed and kissed and kissed—at first standing up, and then we lay down on the bed. I was feeling things I had never felt before. I wanted time to stop and to be with him, in his arms, with his lips on mine, forever. It was that kind of feeling. I love my husband—but this, this feeling is one I have never, ever had.

The clothes started to peel off one item at a time. He wanted to feel me, and I him. I couldn't get enough of his breath, his touch, his kiss, his caress, his everything. We were soon naked, holding each other, exploring and touching. Our kisses led to other parts of our bodies, and we took each other in our mouths and tasted each other over and over.

We spent hours that day in that room, with jets roaring past our hotel window, talking, laughing, sharing, and loving. It was a day that is pressed into my memory and my heart for always.

I truly believe things happen for a reason. I believe that one of the reasons for my getting on Facebook is that it was meant for Ross and me to reconnect. I don't know what the future holds for us—we are both married to other people. I do know that my life will never be the same. I know that the love, the light, the happiness, the joy, that he has brought to me have made me into an incredible woman. I know we cannot be to-gether right now, not in the way we want, but just to have him in my life is a gift.

Ross and I have met several times since that day, and each time has been more intense than the last. When we do see each other, we know we can't deny how we feel. It's incredible—powerful and indescribably passionate. What we have can only be described as one word. . .amazing.

About the Author

Marlo Gottfurcht signed up for a Facebook account almost three years ago. Over 600 friends later, she realized that she was using the site more and more to interact with old friends and to find what she was looking for—a sense of identity, individuality, and excitement. With Facebook, she found support and a new optimism about her future. It also gave her a sense of empowerment to realize that her own marriage was ending.

Marlo grew up in Los Angeles, attended Beverly Hills High School, and graduated with a degree in Communications from Loyola Marymount University. After stints as an associate editor at *Live!* magazine and studying to be a pastry chef, she took a break from the professional world to raise her family.

Marlo is a minivan-driving mom of two children, newly divorced, and a big Facebook fan. She uses it to communicate, reconnect, share, network, poke people—and, of course, for a little flirting of her own.

www.ingramcontent.com/pod-product-compliance
Lightning Source LLC
Chambersburg PA
CBHW051237050326
40689CB00007B/957